The
SILENT
MASTER

The
SILENT
MASTER

Awakening the Power Within

Grandmaster Tae Yun Kim

NEW WORLD LIBRARY
SAN RAFAEL, CALIFORNIA

©1994 Grandmaster Tae Yun Kim

Published by New World Library
58 Paul Drive
San Rafael, CA 94903

Cover Design: Beth Hansen
Text Design & Typography: TBH Typecast, Inc.
Cover Photo: Richard Fuller

Library of Congress Cataloging-in-Publication Data
Kim, Tae Yun.
    The silent master / Tae Yun Kim,
        p. cm.
    ISBN 1-880032-41-4 : $10.95
        1. Self-actualization (Psychology)   2. Centering (Psychology)
3. Centering (Psychology) — Problems, exercises, etc.
4. Meditation — Psychological aspects.   I. Title.
    BF637.S4K544 1994
    158'. 1 — dc20   93-46044
                                                            CIP

ISBN: 1-880032-41-4
First Printing: April 1994
Printed in the U.S.A. on acid-free paper
Distributed by Publishers Group West

10   9   8   7   6   5   4   3   2   1

CONTENTS

ix

Foreword

xiii

Introduction

1

CHAPTER ONE

Freedom! The Goal of Self-Discovery

What is self-discovery? What is your true self? What is freedom? Here, we discuss four basic stages of self-discovery: readiness, energizing, life examination, and rebirth. Meditation.

29

CHAPTER TWO

Readiness: Take Charge of Your Life

Self-discovery happens inside the arena of your consciousness. Have a large "empty cup" as you get ready to discover your true self, and develop the power of your will, motivation, and attitude. Practice. Meditation.

53

CHAPTER THREE

Energizing: Building Creative Power

What is energy? How is energy creative? We look at how to use your two greatest energy tools: purified thought and emotion. Put energy in action with your power of concentration and visualization. Practice. Meditation.

81

CHAPTER FOUR

Life Examination: Defining Your True Self

Does your present life reflect your true priorities? Is your present identity your original self or a copy of others' expectations? Here we look at five ways to re-identify yourself with your true self. Practice. Meditation.

109

CHAPTER FIVE

Rebirth: Living Your True Self

Living as your true self is a life of Love that overcomes all obstacles and brings lasting peace and joy. We look at how to love yourself so that you overcome weaknesses and successfully win your goals. Practice. Meditation.

139

CHAPTER SIX

Freedom: Taking Action!

All journeys begin with the first step. When you're ready to change your life, when you're ready for freedom, you must take action. Here are several key action steps that bring power and freedom. Meditation.

ACKNOWLEDGMENTS

Today, I am still a student, as well as a Grandmaster. Every person who comes into my life teaches me. Each one is a unique individual with something special to give the world. I thank God for the opportunity to help my students uncover their true inner strengths and abilities.

My special thanks go to master instructor Scott H. Salton, senior instructors William H. Hewson, Michael B. Fell, David K. Pariseau, Thomas C. Saunders, and Daniel Johnson for putting forward their dedication, support, and commitment.

To my second-generation junior instructors Mark Amador, Erika Sommers, Kristina Williams, Chase Lang, and Jacklyn Marie, I thank them for their trust in me and their commitment to themselves.

Finally, I want to thank all my students who put their energy together as *one universal mind, one strength, one power, and one healing force.* With the power of this unity there are no obstacles we cannot overcome.

Thank you all.

FOREWORD

Grandmaster Tae Yun Kim teaches far more than martial arts; she teaches fundamentally about *life* — about living life to its fullest, living with joy and love, living with peace and purpose.

Grandmaster's lessons are about rising above the distractions, temptations, and negative forces in our environment. They are about overcoming the disquieting feelings within us — anger, fear, loneliness, self-doubt, and the endless list of negative, self-destructive emotions we commonly experience — in order to let our *real* selves shine through and achieve our goals in this life.

When we accomplish these things, we feel the deep satisfaction that only success can bring. Grandmaster's mission is to help us discover our true power, experience total freedom, and know that success. She is here to do whatever it takes to help her students achieve that special, personal breakthrough.

Grandmaster is a superb communicator — a consummate storyteller who can captivate audiences, entertain them, enlighten them, make them laugh, and touch their hearts, time after time.

She sleeps only a couple of hours each night, and every waking moment is spent fulfilling her purpose — teaching classes, reading letters, reading journals, and meditating for creative inspiration on how to help her students. Sometimes she will call a student with advice, encouragement, or, when necessary, a kick in the rear.

Despite her rigorous schedule, Grandmaster radiates the beauty and vitality of a woman less than half her age, because she has mastered the subject of *energy* — how to separate it, how to channel it, how to focus it. Whatever she does, she does with total focus and concentration. These qualities make her a superb student of human nature. The lessons she has learned in that pursuit are the tools she uses to reach people and to help them. She shares many of those lessons in this volume.

Grandmaster was born to war, poverty, and hunger in her native Korea. Her earliest memories are too painful for most of us to even want to recall. But one of Grandmaster's symbols is the Lotus flower — a flower that rises only out of murky, dirty water, uses that water for nourishment and strength, and then shines forth its beauty for all to see.

Grandmaster is just such a flower. She has harnessed every negative experience in her past and has put it to work for her — to teach her, make her strong, and help her bring forth her inner beauty. Her fundamental lesson is that we have that ability, too. She teaches directly in these pages and indirectly by her example. One is as important as the other. She demonstrates that her principles *work*, and that they can lead us, too, to a life filled with joy, peace, and purpose.

— Eric Armstrong
Milpitas, CA

NOTE:

Discerning readers will notice that the "Silent Master" images that open each chapter are out of order: "Silent Master Image I" opens Chapter One, yet "Silent Master Image III" opens Chapter Two.

The six Silent Master images were first published in Grandmaster's book, *Seven Steps to Inner Power,* and we wished to retain the original numbering of the images, while applying them to different chapters in *The Silent Master.*

INTRODUCTION

As part of my teaching, I hold Self-Discovery Weekends where people explore and express themselves through many different energizing activities. The purpose of these weekends is to give people an opportunity to open up, to love themselves in a more expansive way, and most importantly, to discover more of their true Self. Most of each weekend is spent outdoors in beautiful, remote areas of nature.

I remember that during one of these weekends, while everyone was seated in a circle after completing some breathing exercises, a large butterfly flew into the circle and alighted on my arm.

This charming and fascinating visitor seemed to have a mission. I invited him to step on my hand, and he did so without making any gesture to leave. He stretched his beautiful wings and waved them gently at everyone who came close to look. Even when I stood up and moved around, he still didn't fly away.

Like the butterfly, we had a mission as well. We were gathered together on this day for the purpose of true self-discovery. It seemed as though this beautiful little visitor came to say, "Look at me if you want to know about self-discovery." Perhaps his mission was to remind us of the powerful symbol nature gives us when a lowly, drab caterpillar transforms itself into a multicolored winged being. No longer bound to crawl upon the earth, an altogether different creature flies to the air in freedom!

But imagine if some terrible spell were to make the caterpillar forget his destiny, or forget who he really is. Imagine that the caterpillar never took steps to make the transformation possible. Imagine that he never ate the proper leaves, nor spun the cocoon. Perhaps he spent the rest of his life simply crawling around and avoiding his enemies, finally dying of starvation or old age. What a loss this would be! We would only hope that something, somewhere, sometime would make the caterpillar remember his true identity and fulfill his true destiny.

In the same way, you have the potential to transform a life that is drab, unhappy, limited, or without fulfillment into one that brings the freedom of a butterfly! I call this self-discovery. But self-discovery is really self-rediscovery. You already possess a powerful, pure, and radiant consciousness, which I call the Silent Master. The rediscovery of this aspect of yourself can bring you the freedom that makes life worth living, so that you need not avoid, hide from, or fake life anymore.

In my first book, *Seven Steps to Inner Power*, I present a foundation of principles that lead to the discovery of your Silent Master. Yet once you know about the Silent Master within, when you know who you are and what your potential is, there is one more vital step to take. *Action!* Inner knowledge brings freedom only when you put it into action. In this book, I emphasize how to create your own path of self-discovery so that your knowledge brings you freedom and love and joy.

Something else comes with this territory: *Work!* Self-discovery, taking action, and staying on your path until you reach your goal — all these take work. There's no way around it. Work takes effort! I can tell you honestly I haven't yet met anyone seeking true self-discovery who didn't have obstacles to overcome. But obstacles and mistakes are your friends and teachers. They come to you in exactly the strength you need to build equal strength for overcoming them.

I had to learn this lesson of the butterfly the hard way when I was a young girl studying with my Master in Korea. For many weeks I had been watching a cocoon, waiting for the butterfly to emerge. It was hard to believe that there was any kind of life in there, and I even wondered if maybe the cocoon was dead. My Master assured me much was happening that I couldn't see. "Learn to be patient . . . watch," he said.

One day I thought I saw the tiniest of movements. Putting my ear up to the cocoon, I was startled and thrilled to hear the small scratching sounds of the butterfly within. After so much waiting, it was happening! Finally I was going to see a butterfly emerge. But it seemed to be taking forever. Although I waited for many hours, it still didn't seem able to break out of its cocoon. I decided that it must be having trouble and that I'd better help it. Very carefully I peeled away the outer layer of the cocoon to set the butterfly free. The butterfly did step out, but it couldn't fly! It was just able to walk and flutter. When I called to my Master for help, he saw at once what I had done without me telling him. I had interfered with the butterfly's process. The *effort* — the work — to break out of the cocoon was a necessary part of the butterfly's transformation. In my ignorance, I took away the work necessary to prepare for a life of flying.

In self-discovery, work is a joyful process! Yes, it involves effort, and it involves changing yourself. It may involve doing "scary" things for the first time, and it involves some sacrifice. But the word *sacrifice* comes from a root that means "to make holy." Sacrifice is not real loss. In discovering your true self, you will never lose anything you need, and you will gain only what makes you more pure and more free!

Your work is uniquely yours. No one can do your work or your living for you — no one can know your truth. Even the blade of grass must move the earth by itself. But the single little blade *does* move the earth! The truth is, all your struggles, all your obstacles, all your mistakes are destined to end in victory, not defeat. The powerful presence within you — your Silent Master — is the force of Love. And this Love desires above all to bring you to your highest potential. Love brings you every situation, every obstacle, and every lesson that you need to create your greatest growth.

My own life certainly has not been free of obstacles. To reach my goal of becoming a Grandmaster, I had to overcome the hardships of war and many centuries of limiting prejudice towards women living in Asia.

Today, and every day, I still have many problems to overcome in continuing my work to train others in the art of Jung SuWon (which I translate and define in Chapter One). One purpose of this book is to share with you the action steps that have helped me win my goals. I have never regarded defeat as an acceptable alternative. If defeat has any purpose, it is only to act as a guidepost, as feedback, while you keep moving toward your goal.

If you have tried before — and failed — try again! In this book, I will be asking you to try it my way. I can only tell you that my principles have worked for me and worked for my students. If you are willing to take action, they will work for you too. I have included many action steps in this book to help you create your own path. Keep a pencil handy as you read, and do some of the exercises. Give it a chance — you can always go back to your own way, if you want to.

Remember that you are not alone. Like a single blade of grass, you are one with the Life Force of the universe, and you have the power and ability to fulfill your dreams. My greatest wish is to help you discover the true Love within you, and show you how to use It in creating a life of fulfillment, peace, and joy.

— Grandmaster Tae Yun Kim

The
SILENT
MASTER

CHAPTER ONE

FREEDOM!
THE GOAL OF SELF-DISCOVERY

SILENT MASTER IMAGE I

YOU ARE ONE OF A KIND

Your Silent Master is your Real Self, your original Self. It expresses Itself through your thinking, through true Ideas and Thoughts in your mind. It is your eternal Selfhood that exists apart from your brain (which is a sensory processor only) and the personality traits imposed on you from your environment.

FREEDOM IS YOUR BIRTHRIGHT

You were born to be free! Just as nature is full of wildlife that is born in freedom, you, too, are meant to live free. You are a part of nature, too. And there is no greater freedom than to be the master of your own destiny. There is no greater happiness than to be who you are in truth — not a copy or an imitation of someone else, but rather your own original self.

When you know who you are, you experience yourself as unique, as one-of-a-kind. You have a special place and a special purpose in being here. No one can take your place in life or in the universe. When you know who you really are, you become free because you realize you can be in charge of your life. You learn to use the natural power within you to realize your true desires, to set meaningful goals for yourself, and to fulfill them successfully.

Ask yourself these questions: Have the past five years of your life brought you what you want in life? Were you focused on a goal and going somewhere special? Or were you just drifting, only to find out today, five years later, that your time was mostly wasted?

Maybe you've never asked these questions before, so you might reply without thinking, "I guess I have what I want." Or, maybe you know right now your answer is, "Are you kidding? No way!" Think about it and ask yourself *now*. Are you really excited about getting up every morning? Do you have a career that fulfills you? Do you have love in your life? Do you have a warm and peaceful feeling inside that makes you glad just to be alive, no matter what?

Or do you have a vague feeling that you're somehow "faking it" in your life, as though you've never really known who you are, or all you can do, or why you're here? Do you have a feeling that you've missed really *living* your life, that you're just doing what you can to survive?

When you have your answer, here's something else to keep in mind: the next five years will be just the same — unless you make a change. So you need to ask another question right now: Do I want the next five years to be like the last five?

SELF-DISCOVERY MEANS LEARNING TO LIVE FREE

If your answer to that question is no, then you are ready to begin a journey of self-discovery. The feeling of "faking it" or "missing it" comes from not knowing who you really are. When you discover your true self, you feel the natural desires and aspirations that will guide you into a happy and fulfilling life. You come to know a peace and joy that lives with you no matter what your material circumstances are.

Our thoughts and feelings are pure energy. Whatever we think about consciously and subconsciously manifests in our daily life in one form or another. This means that all the negative thoughts, self-limitations, and doubts we have about ourselves will hold us back from reaching our true self, the person we were born to be. On the other hand, positive attitudes, constructive action, and the pure thoughts and feelings we have will create a very different life of peace and freedom. So, on the journey of discovering your true self, one of the most important tools you'll take with you is your attitude.

The true goal of self-discovery is to find freedom and happiness. If you are not happy right now, if you do not have the freedom you desire, it's only because you're not aware of the power within you to joyfully fulfill your meaningful goals and true desires. Freedom means you don't have to be a victim of your environment. Whatever the circumstances you are born into, or whatever circumstances develop around you as you go through life, freedom means you use your power to take charge of your life and direct your path. And yes, you do have the power!

Some aspects of life are unavoidable. You didn't choose the family or the environment into which you were born, for example. You didn't choose many of the abuses, conflicts, or crises that may have occurred over the years. And you will inevitably experience sickness in some form, old age, and death. But you don't have to regard these things as excuses for continuing unhappiness and failure. Instead, you can decide that right now you will produce change in your life and that you will live your life as fully as you can, with as much love and happiness as you can.

Life is such a precious gift. But we tend to treat every day as though life is never going to end, as though we have an unlimited amount of time to find the happiness we want. As a result, instead of challenging our fears *right now*, we go on day after day, year after year, making excuses for our failure to accomplish our true desires. Good intentions don't seem to be enough to make big changes in your life. Think about all the New Year's resolutions you've made in the past, and you realize that good intentions alone aren't sufficient to introduce changes. Making real and lasting change requires that you make a commitment and take constructive action!

Unfortunately, we tend to get comfortable with our fears and limitations. Think about those times when your eyes adjusted to a semi-dark room. You thought you could see well enough in the darkness. But when the light went on, you suddenly realized how dark it had been. And didn't the light also hurt? It was uncomfortable to adjust to the new light. In the same way, we can get so used to the darkness of our fears, and so comfortable, that we come to prefer the darkness of fear over the light of our true self and true happiness. Then we may find ourselves drifting from day to day

with an attitude that says, "Maybe tomorrow — or maybe someday — my life will work out."

But our time on this earth is eventually going to end. We
don't have an unlimited amount of time to simply wait for
"someday" to come along. In fact, none of us knows the exact
amount of time left in our lives. The willingness to wait end-
lessly for someday causes us to waste precious time and pre-
vents us from taking action that could truly bring about the
good we desire.

HOW DID YOU GET
WHERE YOU ARE NOW?

Self-discovery is delayed for many of us because we have
preconceived images of ourselves that cause us to act in certain ways. This self-image influences the choices we make
about our physical appearance, our career choices, the people we associate with, and the environment in which we
choose to live. All these choices, plus many others, work
together to produce our self-concept. For instance, people
who believe they are ugly and not smart will tend to dress
sloppily, walk around with a slouched posture, and choose a
job that doesn't require much thinking or education. Their
self-concept of being no good will not allow them to be open
to better opportunities.

Your self-concept is largely a product of elements in your
environment. Whatever you see, hear, smell, taste, and feel in
your environment moment by moment encourages you to
make judgments about yourself. Your five senses are constantly tuned in to negative situations that produce a negative self-concept. I sometimes refer to the senses as the "five
thieves," because these negative perceptions rob you of your
natural birthright of true self-knowledge, self-esteem, and

natural joy. And then the process works in reverse: the negative judgments you inflict upon yourself as a result of your environment encourage you to choose or maintain a negative environment. In my teaching, I show how people can be unfairly limited by this connection between environment and self-concept, and how they must improve both simultaneously in order to create good changes in their lives.

Just as your environment has helped to create your self-concept, so has the pattern and quality of your thinking. Of course, there are times when we make an effort to think positively, regardless of conditions in our environment. But a lot of negative thinking slips by us — sometimes silently — in the way we talk to ourselves. "I can't do this," we think to ourselves, "I'll never be able to do that, I'll always be fat, I'm too shy to speak up, I can't sing...." Strongly believing these things, we never give ourselves the opportunity to discover who we really are. We rarely stop and question our assumptions. Are we really this way? Where did these thoughts come from? When did we start believing these things, and why?

When I tell people who are too shy to speak in front of others that they may be mistaken about their lack of ability, they may say, "You're wrong. The proof that I'm too shy is that I can't do it!" Or I might hear, "The proof that I can't sing is that I can't sing!" Or, "The proof that I'm poor in school is that I get poor grades!"

But that isn't proof at all. Here's what it really is: Somewhere, some time, they started *believing* those assumptions. There are lots of reasons why. Usually the reasons go back to a person, a group, or an authority figure, like a parent or teacher or relative. When you're young and dependent, you usually accept what authority figures tell you, and you create your personality and expectations for yourself based on these outside opinions.

When you're young, you don't have the freedom to simply leave your environment, and you probably don't have the power to change it. When you become an independent adult, however, you *can* exercise the power of choice to make changes. An unfortunate past is never an excuse to continue negative thinking in the present. The power to produce change depends on making choices right now — in spite of the past — that lead to achieving your goals.

YOUR REAL SELF IS
THE SILENT MASTER CONSCIOUSNESS

You possess a consciousness within you that I call the Silent Master. Your Silent Master is the part of you that is connected to the same creative Life Force that made the universe. This consciousness works creatively to form your life and your world when you act in harmony with it.

There are six Silent Master images that describe who you truly are. The first image, at the beginning of this chapter, says that your Silent Master is "your Real Self, your original Self." This means that you're an original! You never have to be a copy of someone else. You were born for a special purpose, with all the abilities and attributes you need to fulfill that purpose and to completely be who you are. Let's call this original self your true self. This original self does not feel itself to be shy or believe it can't sing. This self knows it has unlimited intelligence.

How do you discover your true purpose, and where do you find your true self? The Silent Master image answers this question: "It expresses Itself through your thinking, through true Ideas and Thoughts in your mind. It is your eternal self-hood that exists apart from your brain. . . ." You find your Silent Master in your own mind, where you hold thoughts and feelings. You are your true self when your thoughts and feelings come from the purity of your Silent Master consciousness, and not from the many limited beliefs you've been calling your "self."

Your Silent Master is your original self that existed before you started building your personality traits. This pure self is your own mind, and as you tune in to this part of yourself, you become aware of some simple truths. Let's take a look at some of them.

You Express the Qualities of Your Silent Master

Your Silent Master consciousness is pure creative energy. Because It is your mind, *you* possess creative energy as well. Your Silent Master is a mind of ideas that turns ideas into physical forms. So when you hold those ideas, you become a co-creator with life and help manifest those ideas into form with your mind. Because your Silent Master is pure love, it does not contain ideas that harm, hurt, or destroy. You are naturally one with this love, and you can have ideas that build and create, with feelings of joy, peace, and harmony.

Your Silent Master is not something mysterious or far away. It's as close as your own mind because it *is* your own mind. In self-discovery you begin to see which ideas proceed from your Silent Master and which "ideas" are coming from your limited self-concept. You can choose to create forms that bring true happiness and true fulfillment instead of forms that end in self-sabotage and self-destruction.

For example, one of my students was working in a very low-paying factory job in which he was bored and unhappy. When I asked him why he was there, he replied that he "couldn't do what he wanted to do." Having this belief, he was afraid to even try something else. It turned out that what he wanted to do — work with computers — simply required specialized training he hadn't accomplished.

His belief that he "couldn't do what he wanted to do" was simply a limited belief — nothing more. By examining and questioning that fear, he was able to prove that his true self was far more unlimited than his self-concept was. Then, by getting the training and developing a plan of action, he was finally able to obtain the job and salary he desired. In a matter of a few years — and lots of hard work — his salary climbed from $18,000 to $70,000. But even more importantly, along with the process he gained the self-confidence and self-esteem that had been missing. How he felt about himself had changed. His self-image had changed. Feeling differently about himself, he was therefore better able to communicate his ideas to people, and they now responded to him quite differently, with more respect. This is a good example of how self-discovery creates freedom.

You may ask, If my Silent Master — my true self — is already what I am, why do I not know it? Why is my life not automatically perfect and happy?

Because you have free will, you can look away from truth and hold any idea you wish in your consciousness. Your free will allows you to stay in any environment you wish, even one that hurts you. The student just mentioned, for example, was free to believe that he couldn't have the career he wanted and free to work in a boring, limited job that didn't utilize his true abilities. But he was also free to change that belief and to put his true talents to work, and he did just that.

Your Own Thoughts Can Be Your Worst Enemy

What do you keep in your mind most of the time? Isn't it true we are mainly focused on our physical self and our physical life? Thinking about a spiritual self that seems to be outside the concerns of your physical life may seem impractical and unrealistic. But when we understand that this spiritual self is the creative energy behind our lives, we might take a different attitude!

Discovering your Silent Master gives you power to shape your life and create your world far beyond your physical powers. In so doing, you can change from feeling passive, vulnerable, and stagnant to feeling joyous, free, and creative.

Most of us are so preoccupied with our physical pursuits — our marriages, our jobs, the kids' education, politics, the evening news, the economy, and so on — that we don't think in terms of self-development, much less self-discovery. If we don't understand how we are responsible for creating our environment, we may not feel motivated to take responsibility for the quality of our thinking. We may vaguely feel that the world is just "out there," and we try our best just to survive. We may feel isolated, unimportant, and separate, believing that we have no real or significant role to play in the world. Sometimes it isn't until a tragedy or illness strikes that we are motivated to dig deeper into who we really are and what we can accomplish.

Self-discovery is actually going on all the time, whether you realize it or not. With or without tragedy or illness, every minute of your life is some sort of self-discovery. That's because everything you think, say, and do every minute reflects your present concept of yourself. *Your life is a picture of who you think you are.* How very important, then, to *know* who you really are.

Body, Mind, and Spirit Are One

The translation of *Jung SuWon* is "body, mind, and spirit as one." This concept of unity stands behind one of the basic elements of Jung SuWon teaching, namely:

The best material self you can be
is always a picture of
your True Self,
your pure spiritual being.

Your material self is a reflection of your true self because they are one and the same! Because you are reading this book, you most likely have made the choice to discover the truth about yourself and your life. We will be looking at ways to purify and strengthen your mind so it can bring forth the forms you desire in the purest and best way.

Your body, as well as everything you experience, is influenced by your thoughts and emotions. The more purely and truly your thoughts and emotions mirror your Silent Master consciousness, the more effectively you can respond to any limiting factors or obstacles. You will learn to use the power of your mind to make choices and take actions that create the changes and improvements you wish to see in your body and environment.

THE SEVEN STEPS TO SELF-DISCOVERY

If your life is not filled with things that are as pure and true as you'd like them to be, be assured that even these negative pictures have a purpose. The negatives in your life simply show you where your thinking can be corrected, where your beliefs need to be examined, and where you can take positive action to change your environment. Any disharmony, illness, limitation, unhappiness, or tragedy is an opportunity to open to the reality of your true self, to tap into your ever-present Silent Master consciousness within. It's an opportunity to start on a journey of true self-discovery.

And what are the goals of this journey? The discovery of peace and joy. The discovery of inner power, healing, and freedom! Whatever path develops for you when you make the decision to discover your true self starts you on the way to the goal of freedom.

There are seven qualities — or principles — that are the foundation of the path of self-discovery. No matter how your path progresses or whatever conditions you develop, these principles remain the same for everyone. They are the basis of all creative power. These qualities are: *body and mind as one, truth, purity, love, loyalty, sacrifice, and patience.* In developing these qualities, you bring your Silent Master consciousness to bear on all aspects of your life. Your Silent Master consciousness is a mover and a shaper, and because you are one with this consciousness, you have freedom to reshape or transform your life.

We first work to bring our *body and mind as one* so that we can apply and focus ourselves to learning. So often we are distracted and unfocused; to dedicate ourselves to self-discovery, we must unite our whole being in this task.

Our second step inward is to seek the *truth* in ourselves and in the world around us. We look at who we really are, not who others say we are. This introspection helps us to discover both our strengths and our weaknesses. It also allows us to discover what our real goals are. As we glimpse who we are, we discover the things we want to change in order to become who we want to be.

The third step is *purity.* As we recognize our fears and weaknesses, we build the desire to remove these impurities. Our goal is to purify our bodies, minds, and spirits from the chains we've imposed on them from our lifestyles, attitudes, and environment.

The fourth step is to learn to love ourselves with a pure, accepting, and spiritual *love.* We build on ourselves — overcoming our weaknesses, developing our strengths, discovering our potential. As we see ourselves through our inner eyes, a growing sense of beauty and acceptance forms within us, ultimately leading to inner peace and self-contentment.

This love for ourselves multiplies our self-worth and makes our goals and development become priorities, so we develop a *loyalty* to ourselves and our growth, to our beliefs, our purpose, and our path.

Sacrifice is the sixth principle in our lives: to eliminate unnecessary activities and to make decisions about where to spend our energy, time, and money so that we achieve our goals. We realize that many of the things we originally thought would be sacrifices turn out to be distractions side-tracking us from our ultimate goals.

Finally, we develop *patience*. Through the growing pro-cess of self-discovery we become more patient with ourselves and others. We learn to be content with the path we choose, our direction, and our progress. We stop living for tomorrow and live and breathe the journey right now, weathering life's surprises and disappointments, remaining at peace with our direction and ourselves.

If you feel unfulfilled, out of place, or generally unhappy, your disharmony may be telling you that you are not on your true path. There could be many reasons why you may have taken a path in life leading you away from rather than toward your true purpose. But the truth and purpose of your being, as well as all the mental, emotional, and physical tools you need for action, are here right now in your Silent Master con-sciousness. Who you are in truth is available right now for you to know. Right now, this minute, you can make a decision to commit to your true self, to find your real power, purpose, and life.

Sometimes there are powerful environmental obstacles to overcome when you seek true self-discovery. If this is so for you, then you may have to work hard to overcome them. Self-discovery is not necessarily easy, but difficulty is not a reason to abandon your goals. What does it matter if overcoming obstacles is difficult? When you reach your goal, the difficulties settle in the dust behind you as you enjoy your success.

I had to overcome centuries of prejudice against women in my country just to devote my life to martial arts. Everything in my Korean cultural environment said it was impossible for a woman to become a martial arts master, let alone a grandmaster. Women were supposed to cook and sew and look after children. The pressure to conform to this "law" was enormous. But I did not listen to that, and instead focused all my energy on my goals. I succeeded. When I came the United States, I had more obstacles to overcome — learning to live in a different country and establishing my school. But again, I worked until I succeeded. Even today I have more goals and, therefore, more obstacles. But I use my understanding of Jung SuWon to help me build my life and to help others develop using the same principles.

THE FOUR STAGES
OF SELF-DISCOVERY

Self-discovery is going on every moment of your life. The question is, Are you sitting in the driver's seat? That is, are you guiding the process so that you discover a self that has freedom, energy, and love? Or are you discovering a more limited self every day?

I have learned that there are four basic stages in true self-discovery. These stages may recycle over and over again as you grow and rise to higher levels of knowing yourself. As a tree grows, doesn't it create more than one branch? To some extent, the stages may overlap or happen at the same time. But for the sake of discussion, we can talk about them separately to see what the main challenges are at each stage.

I call the four stages of self-discovery *readiness, energizing, life examination, and rebirth*. We will discuss these stages in depth in the following chapters, but for now let's define them.

1. Readiness

There's a story about a rabbit who fell into a deep hole in the woods. He hopped up and down inside the hole time after time after time, trying so hard to get out, but never succeeding. Many other woodland animals came and watched this show, feeling sorry for the rabbit and expressing all kinds of sympathy and concern. But, of course, that was no help. Finally they all left. The next day when they returned to continue watching, they found the rabbit sitting calmly by a tree covering the hole. "You got out!" they exclaimed in amazement. "How did you do that?" "Well," the rabbit replied, "there was this big tree falling down over the hole, and so . . . I *had* to."

And so it is that many of us aren't ready to discover our spiritual nature until we feel we have to. Suddenly you may have a life-threatening illness, or perhaps experience some kind of loss. At those times you generally feel the need to search for a way to cope and for a deeper meaning to life. You naturally turn within yourself, looking and listening for a feeling of something true and real. That something is your real self, your Silent Master consciousness.

That is why adversity can be a blessing in disguise. It turns you to your true self, where you not only find healing, but more of your undiscovered potential as well.

Whatever your motive for seeking your real self, you must be willing to do four things if you are ready to seek and find your true self. You must be:

> *Willing to commit*
> *Willing to change*

Willing to have an open mind
Willing to take action

Commitment

Here's an illustration I use when talking to students about the importance of commitment and of setting priorities at the beginning of their journeys:

Imagine that you are lost and alone in a fiery hot desert, the sun beating down on you as you trudge through the burning sands. You've gone for days with no food and little water, and your body is weak from exhaustion and exposure. Heat waves are rising in front of you, blurring your vision, and there is nothing but hot, dry sand all around you.

What's on your mind? What are you thinking about? Are you still worried about what color you're going to paint the kitchen?

Most likely there is only one thought in your mind, and that is getting what you need for survival: water. Desperately you need water. Only this thought keeps you moving and keeps your feet wading through the scorching sands. Whatever else you may have wanted at other times in your life pales in comparison to this single goal.

All that's left in your mind is the thought of an overwhelming thirst, a need for the one substance that will save your life. What are you willing to give in order to get it? What are you willing to sacrifice in order to get it? Aren't you resolved to commit all your resources at the present moment to get water — the thing that will save your life?

Suddenly you come to a patch of sand that's darker, harder, and firmer than the rest. Your heart beats faster with anticipation as your mind contemplates the possibility that water is there. You fall to your knees and tear at the sand, digging deeper and deeper as your fingers scratch and bleed. Then the sand becomes moist and you feel within yourself a burst of energy that you didn't know was possible. With renewed strength, you dig faster and harder until you feel the cool liquid on your hand, and you take it and splash it quickly into your parched mouth.

This story is a picture of how priorities form. In a situation like this, you become completely focused on what you want and what you need! This is what I mean by commitment. Are you in some kind of desert situation in your life right now? Are there situations in your life that stubbornly resist solutions? Then you will need to look for the solution with the same commitment as the person in the desert did.

In your imagination you were totally committed to the goal of finding water. As a result, you found it! Were you thinking of the pizza parlor during your search? Your girlfriend or boyfriend? The movie you saw last week? No, you had no distractions, just the commitment to find water and the perseverance to keep going until the goal was won.

In the same way, when you decide you want to find your true self, you will need to commit to the process. In your imagination, your commitment to find water was forced on you by circumstances. Like the rabbit in the previous story, you had to find water or die! Although this seems like an extreme example, your need to know your real self can be just as great. Even if you don't have a life-threatening situation that could be healed only by the power of your real self, it would be a terrible waste to let your life slip away without realizing your full potential.

Change

Next, after commitment, you must be willing to change. You must be willing to become a new person, a different person. And you must be willing to give up old concepts of yourself even before you see your new qualities. The autumn leaves must fall before spring can bring new growth. Death of the old is necessary to prepare for the new.

I love watching children because they can teach us so much about the process of learning. They are focused when they learn something new, as they drink in every drop of information. Why do we so often stop learning and growing as we become adults? Why is it so much more difficult? Isn't it because we stop questioning or examining what's around us? We become satisfied that we've learned enough. We become comfortable with the habits we've acquired. Some people refer to this concept as the comfort zone, which describes how we tend to hang onto worn-out, ineffective attitudes and habits simply because they're familiar. Things that are familiar don't stimulate or scare us the way new situations might, so we tend not to question familiar patterns. But the price we pay for familiarity is that we stop experiencing and instead repeat old habits over and over.

We also avoid new experiences by being overly judgmental about people and events. We make up our minds ahead of time about how something will be instead of remaining open to the unexpected. But to find a new you, you'll have to put aside all your perceived limitations and problems and look at yourself with new eyes. You will have to look at yourself as if for the first time, with the eyes of a child discovering something new.

An Open Mind

This requires having an open mind. You may have to say, "I don't know all that I am to be, but I know what I am not, and I desire to be rid of my old self. I am willing to try something new."

I call this openness forming an empty cup. This means you are willing to regard your body and your life as an empty vessel ready to be filled with the new. The Bible expresses it in this way:

No one sews a patch of unshrunk cloth on an old garment. If he does, the new piece will pull away from the old, making the tear worse. And no one pours new wine into old wineskins. If he does, the wine will burst the skins, and both the wine and the wineskins will be ruined. No, he pours new wine into new wineskins.

MARK 2:21–22

These words tell us that transforming your life does not mean patching up or fixing the old. It means starting over. It means getting a new vessel to hold a new you. You need a new mind and a new body to create a new life. Sometimes in my classes I bring a full cup of water and show my students what happens when you try to pour new water into a full cup. The full cup simply overflows; it cannot hold anything new.

Have a large empty cup! Let your cup be ready to hold many new things. If we focus only on looking for a pearl, we miss the diamond at our feet. It's good to have a specific goal, but also be willing to receive all kinds of new ideas, new feelings, and new visions. The only way we can ever truly learn something is if we are totally open and receptive. The greatest obstacles to our learning are our own doubts, suspicions, and self-imposed limiting judgments.

Having a large empty cup means you are willing to fill it with anything and everything good, not just one thing. You may start on a self-discovery journey to lose weight, for instance. But if you limit yourself to just that, you may not let your spiritual growth open other avenues for you. In the process of losing weight, for instance, you may develop interests that remind you how much you like reading. What may have begun as a journey to lose weight could end up being a journey to become the librarian you were meant to be and had always wanted to be.

Action

When you are really ready to become new and cast off the old, and when you have accepted that you will necessarily change and are prepared to do so, you must do something about it. We've discussed how good intentions alone are not sufficient to bring about change. You'll have to take action. One way or another you'll have to set a plan in motion. In Chapter Six we will look at numerous actions you can take to reach your goals. At this readiness stage, however, the important thing is the willingness to take action. And perhaps the very first action you take on your journey is to begin the second self-discovery stage of *energizing*.

2. Energizing

The readiness stage is like getting a clean sheet of paper ready to write on. Obviously you don't want to write on paper that's already marked up. You are ready to move further on your self-discovery path when you're open for development, like using the clean sheet of paper. You are then prepared for the next stage: *energizing*.

This stage involves getting your energy under control — purifying it, increasing it, and directing it toward goals and activities that promote your growth and development rather than self-destructive or limited ends. Because you are unique, it is important not to compare yourself with others or have unrealistic expectations for what you want to accomplish. There is already within you a quiet recognition of the goals that are appropriate for you. An unrealistic goal will make you feel "pushed" or anxious, whereas a realistic goal will bring a sense of excitement and eager anticipation.

What *is* energy? Energy is an expression of the Life Force of the whole universe. And you and the Life Force are one! Because you are at one with the Life Force of the universe, you *are* energy. And the sun, wind, water, and all of nature are also energy. When you cannot find this energy within your-self, often you can go into nature to feel and connect with it. This Life Force — this energy — is Love in action. When you start feeling this natural Love within you, it will change how you see and respond to the whole world. You will start feeling a warmth, buoyancy, and enthusiasm that flows out of you as naturally as breathing.

One of the goals of self-discovery is to be able to enjoy this natural energy of Love and share it with everyone. Yet why do we often feel such a lack of energy if we are indeed one with the Life Force behind the whole universe? The answer is that our own negative thoughts, attitudes, and emotions act like filters that keep this mighty river of energy down to a trick-ling stream. One purpose of the Jung SuWon training is to purify these filters — to purify your thinking and feeling — so that energy flows more freely and powerfully.

For example, one of the black-belt instructors in my school told me how his teaching changed when he began to approach it with this natural Love. Before he began to feel his spiritual energy increasing, his teaching consisted of making sure the students did every move correctly or learned at the proper rate. This is part of being a good teacher, of course. But when he began to feel more of the natural Love within him, his teaching went beyond physical instruction. He listened and responded with more awareness and sensi-tivity to everyone's special needs and unique feelings. He not only desired to see the students learn the correct moves, but he desired to help them defeat their weaknesses and shine with self-confidence and self-esteem. He cared about every step of their growth with as much enthusiasm as he cared about his own growth. In short, he began *loving* the students as well as teaching them, and it made his job more joyous and fulfilling than anything he'd ever known.

That is how Love energizes you. It gives you inner joy, enthusiasm, and awareness that helps you carry out the work of meeting your goals.

Would you be surprised to know that you may be wasting your energy, spending it on things that undermine and sabotage your goals and desires? You may have habits that regularly weaken the quality of your energy. Your energy is a creative tool! It must not be wasted.

When I teach my students to break bricks with their bare feet or hands, I'm teaching them to control and direct their energy in a positive way. Jung SuWon training does not teach only martial arts movements. Because body and mind are one, this physical training helps students contact their spiritual energy. There is always a balance between the two. You can't have a pure body without a pure mind, and vice versa. You may develop your mind, but if you don't take care of or develop your body, it will have an effect on you. When your body gets hurt, doesn't that cloud your thoughts? Likewise, if you pay attention to developing only your physical body and neglect your mental training, you will be unable to deal with life's situations. Body and mind must always work together.

Your whole being — physical, mental, and emotional — is an expression of energy. To create, transform, or reshape your life, then, your energy must be pure and free. And as you purify your energy, you move into the next stage of examining the content of your life.

3. Life Examination

Life examination is the third stage of self-discovery. First, in the readiness stage, you make the commitment to change your life; second, in the energizing stage, you begin the process of purifying and increasing your energy to ensure that you create pure and true forms in your life; and now, in the third stage of *life examination*, you define and prioritize your specific goals so that you have a clear target on your individual path. You take a hard look at your *present* priorities. As you look at your life, ask, "What is the meaning of what I've created as my life?" Or, "Have I been true to myself? Am I where I want to be? Do I know who I am? Am I being who I am, or am I being who somebody else wants me to be?"

Only by looking closely at where you are can you evaluate the quality of your environment, motives, beliefs, and attitudes. You can't change anything until you identify precisely what needs to be changed. The conditions in your environment and the quality of your thinking have brought you to where you are now. Do you like where you are? If not, where did you compromise or sell out along the way? How did you get off the track? And why? What forces did you respond to instead of listening to the quiet truthful knowing of your Silent Master consciousness? Only by looking honestly at where you are now can you form a good plan to go somewhere else. A careful evaluation will help you see where you detoured, help you determine where you want to go now, and plan how you will get there. That is, you will acquire new motives, ideas, and attitudes that will foster a new self-concept and most likely a new environment. As you look at your life, do not underestimate the power of the environment (job, relationships, family, and so on) you are presently in. To what extent is your environment speaking to you more loudly than your own inner desires? Is your environment promoting the awareness of your strengths, or is it smothering you? You cannot assume everyone you know, whether a perceived friend or foe, wants you to change in the ways you want to change.

Help is always available to you, but the help you need may not be easy to find where you are now. Your environment and certain people in it may have to go, or be modified, in order for you to change. If this is true for you, it's important not to become desperate or to make premature moves without thinking things through clearly and thoroughly. Not everyone who promises you help is able to give it. This is when the tools of meditation, concentration, and visualization (which we discuss in Chapter Three) can help you move wisely at the right time.

Life examination is the part of the self-discovery process in which you begin to *redefine* yourself. After looking at how you may have missed the mark, you now mobilize your inner power to recreate your life. All the bad experiences you've had can be used as feedback; they are the fertilizer that enables you to grow strong.

Mistakes can be a good friend to us when we use them as feedback in a learning process. As a Western society, we are terrified of failure. We often feel that mistakes reveal fatal flaws in our character. But when we make mistakes, it is a sure sign we are learning. One of the ways we learn what's right is by learning first what's wrong. As long as we are trying to grow productively and to apply the lessons we learn, our mistakes will surely propel us to success. Alexander Graham Bell, Albert Einstein, Thomas Edison, Abraham Lincoln, and most other persons who achieved something significant failed numerous times before succeeding. But they were also learning before they succeeded, just as you will do. Through your successes and failures you eventually are guided to choose your path and control your destiny.

When you have thoroughly analyzed and evaluated your life and have made the determination to become who you are in truth, you are ready for the next step, rebirth.

4. Rebirth

When you reach *rebirth*, you have already committed to change your life for the better (readiness), you have done much work to purify your mind and body (energizing), and you have set true goals for yourself (life examination). Now you put all of this into action as your new way of life. Rebirth means actually *living* the new definition of yourself. Now, instead of drifting along in life, acting and reacting with limited perception, you live with conscious awareness of your connection to your Silent Master consciousness. You now become your own doctor and surgeon, carefully bringing your new self into the world by constantly removing the strangling, stifling thoughts and feelings of your old self.

Rebirth is not something that happens and then ends. Rebirth is an ongoing process, a daily practice that goes on for your entire life. As you continue to move down your life's path, you will constantly be made aware of changes you need to make and will constantly be reborn as you make them.

You will always be striving to look at yourself impartially, like a doctor examining a patient for the first time — studying the symptoms, trying to gain insight into the source of the trouble, and prescribing the appropriate cure. Only by being willing to constantly look at your weaknesses can you constantly do something about them. This becomes a way of living, and this process requires the inner power steps of love and loyalty: love of your real self, and loyalty to your goals.

Love and loyalty are important, because when you actually start living your Silent Master consciousness, new challenges are guaranteed to arise to test your commitment. The higher a tree rises in the sun, the longer the shadow it casts. The greater your achievement, the greater the tests that come. Some challenges at this stage may appear just as negative as certain experiences prior to the knowledge of your Silent Master. But there will be a difference now, because you will *know* you are not a victim. Now you will *know* your true self is greater and more powerful than anything that threatens to take away your natural joy and freedom.

This is the kind of newness and excitement and discovery you were born to experience. Life is magic in that it unfolds every moment in a new way, darting off in a new, unexpected direction, depending on your focus. But life is also a science, which you can learn to operate and enjoy with exactness and understanding.

To be reborn into your true identity is an exhilarating goal. The prize is worth the price of any effort.

One of the comments I hear many times from the people I work with is that they feel alone, isolated, or separate. If you feel alone and unfulfilled, you probably are trying to be a copy of someone else, or are trying to fulfill expectations of others. Or, perhaps you're trying to find yourself *in* someone else, hiding behind a stronger personality instead of finding your own strong and unique self.

But your true self feels whole and complete whether or not you are alone. The true meaning of *alone* is *all-one*. When you are one with your true self, one with your own Silent Master consciousness, you are one with the universe, one with *all that is*. When you feel your true self, you feel at rest in the wholeness of things, but you also know that you are original and unique. Although you feel yourself as a separate, special individual, you do not feel empty and unfulfilled. You feel true and pure and good and whole. Most importantly, you feel enthusiastic, creative, and joyful. This is the natural state of your true being.

When you are really ready to find this aspect of your being and realize the fullness of your potential, you will begin the process of self-discovery. I honor you. I respect you. That is why I'm sharing with you the teachings of Jung SuWon. Although you and I can begin this journey together, it's still going to be your journey. I can share with you my experiences, my teachings, my hopes and expectations of your successful outcome, but it remains at all times your journey, your commitment, your perseverance, your goal — and your prize!

Since all that you need to know about your real self is within you right now, my wish is to encourage and guide you to the door of your own powerful Being.

Here are some beautiful words from *The Prophet* by Kahlil Gibran, which describe how everyone is individual. We need to love and value and acknowledge the gifts that are uniquely ours.

> *The musician may sing to you of the rhythm which is in all space, but he cannot give you the ear which arrests the rhythm nor the voice that echoes it. . . .*
>
> *For the vision of one man lends not its wings to another man.*
>
> *And even as each one of you stands alone in God's knowledge, so must each one of you be alone in his knowledge of God and in his understanding of the earth.*

But to be alone with the Life Force of the universe is to be one with all that is, and this is certainly not lonely. This is fulfillment.

MEDITATION

Right now I am the Silent Master consciousness, and I can feel Its wholeness and completeness whenever I have a need. I see myself growing. My Silent Master consciousness is present now to help me find my right place and right purpose. Because I am one with the Life Force of the universe, I can feel Love and energy already within me moving me forward. I am unique and individual, yet I am part of the whole. I can achieve my goals. I share what I am, lovingly and givingly, because my unique part to play is necessary to complete the whole. I am alone, yet I am alone with the entire manifest universe and every other individual. Together we are each alone, and together we are all-one, and together we each fulfill our unique purpose in harmony and peace.

CHAPTER TWO

READINESS:
TAKE CHARGE OF YOUR LIFE

SILENT MASTER IMAGE III

YOUR THOUGHTS
CREATE REALITY

Your Silent Master Consciousness knows Itself to be immaterial in substance, but It also takes form (manifests) as your physical body and material world around you. Thus, you may describe yourself as being both immaterial (spiritual) and material (physical) at the same time.

It's really true that you can't learn something new until you want to. I call the desire to learn *readiness*. But even when you sincerely desire to change your life, and feel really ready, you may be surprised at how much energy this change takes at first! As a result, you can easily find ways to put off your efforts indefinitely.

The first step to take in the readiness stage of self-discovery is to take charge of your thinking. Every response you make to your environment, and every action you take (or don't take) is propelled by a decision, choice, or response that you make in your thinking. And the most important aspects of your thinking to take charge of are *will, motivation*, and *attitude*. As we discuss these areas, I will refer to the five principles of mental conduct, which are an important part of the Jung SuWon training. These principles enable you to take charge of your thinking so that your mental activity supports you rather than sabotages you:

1. Identify your fears and weaknesses, and conquer them.
2. Learn from your mistakes.
3. Know that you have the ability to do, the capacity to act, and the capability to perform and produce.
4. Have determination and a quality purpose.
5. Have a positive mental attitude.

WILL

Where Have You Focused Your Will?

When you become ready for something new, you must be *willing* to work toward your goal. Being willing means two things: it means you are open to experience something new, and it means you use your *will* power to focus on that experience and persevere until it is accomplished. When you desire to discover your Silent Master consciousness, your pursuit begins with your will to find it. Your Silent Master consciousness is already within you, but you must seek it actively and with perseverance.

One of the greatest obstacles to achievement that I see is the tendency to give up. Sometimes people want to give up just when they are about to accomplish their goal. When this happens, your best friend is your will power. When I see my students lacking in will power, especially at a critical turning point, I do everything I can to rouse them. "No!" I say. "Don't give up now! You can do it! Finish what you started!" Giving up is such a sad waste after putting in so much effort.

I mentioned before that you might be surprised how much energy it takes to change your life. Since bad habits and negative thinking build up such momentum over time, only your will power can break through and give you the push to get started and to stay on course.

When you realize this, you may be thinking that your self-discovery journey is over! "I have no will power," a lot of people say. To this I say, Yes, you do. In fact, you're using your will power right now to pursue all the bad habits you presently have. No one orders you to hide when it's time to meet new people. No one makes you fail the exam you didn't study for. You do these things by yourself, with the power of your will. What you need to do is learn to use your will power constructively and positively.

Shock Can Mobilize Your Will

Many times your will is automatically mobilized by some kind of shock. But what you think is the worst thing that could happen to you often turns out to be a powerful force for good. This is when the fourth principle of mental conduct needs to be applied: Have determination and a *quality* purpose. When something terrible happens to you, use it to form determination and a purpose. You have a choice as to how you will respond in every situation. You alone determine whether an event will have a positive or negative impact, depending on the quality of your response.

Sometimes we have a tendency to become self-destructive when we are hurt badly, and we take actions that increase and reinforce the hurt. But we do have another option. Using our awareness, we can examine the circumstances in our environment that contributed to our hurt, and we can take action to change them.

In my own life, for instance, a powerful event in my childhood helped me focus my will and gave me a quality purpose to pursue for the rest of my life. During the Korean war, when I was only five years old, my friend and I were running from the shells exploding all around us. As we were running, my friend, also five years old, was blown apart right in front of me. I did not understand war and death at that age — or the shock I felt. But my young mind formed a very strong response: I will never run again. That event was the starting point of a life in which I would strive to develop the strength to confront and overcome destruction, rather than run from it.

Instead of channeling my will power into a response of bitterness and hate, I channeled it into the determination to become a martial artist. This in itself required my constant will to persevere because women in my country were not involved or supported in this pursuit. Even when my mother tried to keep me in my room to prevent me from practicing, I found a way to continue.

Use Your Will to Conquer Fears and Weaknesses

Although some kind of shock is often a common way to rouse will power, it is not the only way. Sometimes you can summon your will simply from an intense desire to overcome stagnant, limited, or stifling circumstances. In this case, you have to be willing to let go of the past, and to let go of your fears and weaknesses. These things have to go because they have kept you from moving in a positive direction. Make the first principle of mental conduct a constant way of life: Identify your fears and weaknesses and conquer them.

Your weaknesses — or bad habits — can become such a part of you that you begin to think they *are* you. Did you ever hear the story of the frog and the scorpion?

Once there was a frog and a scorpion who both wanted to get to the other side of a river. It was no problem for the frog. All he needed to do was jump in and swim to the other side. It was a different story for the scorpion, however, because he had no way to cross the river by himself.

So he asked the frog for help. "Say, Frog, would you be willing to allow me to ride on your back across the river?" he asked earnestly.

"Are you kidding?" the frog answered. "You'll sting me and I'll die! No, I won't help you."

"But wait," the scorpion pleaded. "Just think. If I sting you and you die, then I would die, too! So why would I do something that would hurt both of us?"

The frog thought about it; the scorpion did seem to make sense. Finally, after much hesitation, the frog said reluctantly, "OK, do you promise not to sting me?"

"Of course I promise," the scorpion replied, and happily jumped on the frog's back. So off they went into the river.

But about halfway across, the scorpion began to feel an irresistible urge rising from deep within. Suddenly, without warning, he stung the frog.

"Why did you do that?" the frog exclaimed in stunned amazement. "Do you realize what you've done? Now we're both going to die!"

"I know," the scorpion said.

"But why?" the astonished frog continued to ask. "Why?"

"I'm sorry, I couldn't help it," gurgled the scorpion, sinking below the water. "It's just my nature."

Instead of being inflexible like the scorpion and regarding your bad habits as "just your nature," or "just the way you are," why not try another approach? Let's assume for a moment that your negative traits are beliefs that you have adopted about yourself, and that you can use your will power to begin the process of conquering them. If you have beliefs like "I'm lazy," "I'm shy," "I'm useless," "I'm poor," "I'm stupid," let's ask, What do you get out of these beliefs? If you're holding on to them so tightly, you must be getting something you think you want. But is it happiness you're getting? Success? Achievement? Growth? I really doubt if you're getting anything good from those beliefs.

If you really want to change your life, you may have to see that what you're really getting out of these beliefs is an *excuse* not to face up to some fear or weakness you have. As long as you believe you're lazy, will you focus your will on going to school to learn something new? No, because if your laziness is really a fear of failure, you won't test yourself in school. As long as you believe you're shy, will you use your will power to seek out a new, more fulfilling career in which you have to meet many people? No, because if your shyness is really a fear of talking to others, you'll keep your undesirable present job where there are few people. In both of these situations, you are *afraid*, not really lazy, and not really shy.

But feelings of limitation are so unnecessary. Fear can be conquered! Weakness can be overcome. Each time you use your will power to stand up and throw yourself into the face of another "I can't," you are getting ready for a victory. So, in the readiness stage of self-discovery, you begin to identify your fears and weaknesses, and start to confront them.

Realize That "I Can't" Usually Means "I Won't"

All of us, at some time or another, have felt the limiting power of "I can't." Even when we really want something, and even if that something is within our power, those two simple words can prevent it from happening. When you find your-self saying "I can't," look deeper to see if you're making another excuse. If you look honestly, you will usually find that your words "I can't" actually mean "I could, but I won't for this or that reason." For instance, "I can't do well in school" might easily mean, "I could do well in school, but I won't put in the time and effort to study." When you become willing to say "I can," you find the power to carry it out from your Silent Master within.

Here's a story that illustrates what I mean.

During a war, a group of people was fleeing from the enemy. Among them was an old man and a woman with a baby. For many days they ran and hid, always with the enemy close behind and danger from every corner.

As they ran, others in the group helped the mother carry the baby, except for the old man, who was already very weak.

After a few days the old man was so tired he just couldn't go on. He fell by the side of the road and lay there breath-less. The others stopped to help, but he urged them on, ask-ing them to just leave him there. He had given up all will to live, all desire for life or for the future.

The enemy was fast approaching, so the others were anx-ious to move on. The woman with the baby then looked down at the old man and said, "It's your turn. Everyone else has helped carry the baby. Now it's your turn. You must fulfill your responsibility."

She placed the baby in the old man's lap and went after the others who were hurrying away. Inside, her heart beat terribly for the child, but she kept going. Others in the group wondered why she was just leaving her baby there to die. What kind of mother was she? But still, they all kept moving.

Meanwhile, the old man held the baby, while the sound of the enemy drew nearer. His heart was filled with weariness and despair, yet he was stirred by the baby moving and mumbling next to him. His life had been full and long, with much pain and happiness, and he just felt too tired to go on. But beside him was a little baby who had many years ahead and so much to live for.

He could not just lie there and take that away from the child. Strength and new energy flowed into his veins. He picked up the child and ran as best he could to catch up to the others.

On and on he went with only one thought in his mind: the safety of the child. Nothing else mattered, not fear, weariness, hunger. On and on he ran until in the distance he could see his friends still moving quickly. He was so close, only a little farther to go to reach them.

Before long, he caught up with them, stumbling into their midst with the precious baby, and gasping for breath. The others were amazed at this feat and wondered where he had found the strength to run with the child and catch them. But they could see his face was filled with a resoluteness and determination they hadn't seen before.

Gently, he handed the child to the mother, who took back the little body lovingly. Her heart was filled with joy, both for her child and for the old man. Together they continued onward, away from the enemy until they were safe and secure.

In this story, the old man found that he created two different paths based on two different choices. "I can't" made him fall by the wayside, convinced that his life was at an end — and so it would have been. "I can" enabled him to get up, find strength available within himself, and run to victory.

Both were real and valid possibilities. What made the difference between these two choices? We might say this woman did what a good teacher does. She gave the man an opportunity to discover and demonstrate the strength he had inside. Then the old man did his part. He used his will to conquer his weakness and defeatism. He found the strength within to carry out his mission. He chose how to respond to the opportunity, and used his will to choose victory over defeat.

Although this story shows how one particular situation can be an opportunity to overcome limitation, true and lasting change requires effort that goes beyond just one situation. One victory doesn't solve every problem. To create lasting change, one victory must lead to new ways of thinking and acting.

Regard Mistakes as Teachers, Not Judges

You can also use your will power to employ the second rule of mental conduct: Learn from your mistakes.

So often, when we do something that we believe is a mistake, we become fatalistic and give up our efforts. Instead of focusing on a new direction right away, we tend to sit around in gloom and doom criticizing ourselves. We use mistakes as excuses not to face up to fears and weaknesses.

Rather than allowing your mistakes to be reasons for continuing failure, allow your mistakes to be used as learning feedback. In fact, mistakes are as real and as valid as successes when you're growing and learning.

You make mistakes any time you do something new. If you already knew how to do something without making mistakes, it wouldn't be new! It would already be a habit. So let mistakes be friendly teachers, the fertilizer for growth.

When I say be willing to make mistakes, I mean let your mistakes lead you into new understandings and new actions. As long as you're making different mistakes, you can be sure you're on a path of learning. It's a natural part of the process. Of course, you don't want to keep repeating the same mistakes. If that happens, it's a signal that you're not learning from the mistakes the way you should.

All that you judge to be a *mistake* in your life is nothing more and nothing less than an event that teaches you something. Unfortunately, we usually label our mistakes as bad things that happen, as opposed to good things that happen. But judgments of good and bad are unnecessary. Whatever you call a mistake is really just neutral feedback about the result of a certain direction you've taken. Whether an event or a direction is judged to be good or bad is probably beyond your perception at the moment. To illustrate what I mean, consider the following scenario.

Suppose you're laid off from your job. Bad? But then someone offers you a new job that pays more money. Good? But then you find at this new job you work for a tyrannical boss. Bad? But then the boss retires and turns the business over to you. Good? But then the building catches fire and burns down. Bad? But then you collect insurance money that lets you start the business you always wanted. Good? But then ... but then.... Life in this material dimension will always be a succession of "but thens."

In this example, you can see how all the events taken by themselves are neither good nor bad — even though you may judge them so. They are simply a series of events leading in a certain direction, and all judgments of good or bad are totally irrelevant in the long run. Losing your job in the beginning was not a mistake because it ultimately led you to having the business you always wanted.

How much time we waste in fretting over our mistakes! All this does is keep us dwelling on the past, and this brings the unwanted past into the *present.*

How important it is, then, when you're ready to pursue your Silent Master consciousness, to let go of your mistakes, and use your will to focus on a new direction. Look at your mistakes, see what you have learned, but then let them go.

Will Doesn't Have to Be Struggle

You may have to persist when you are trying to hold onto an idea or a goal you wish to manifest. But persistence doesn't necessarily involve struggle. The exercise of will should be a calm, persistent focus that doesn't allow a feeling of resistance. The exercise of will should not have to be a battle.

If you feel a struggle when you exert your will, there may be old habits or false beliefs you need to let go of. The sense of struggling to hold an idea is a signal to you that you are simultaneously holding an equal, opposite idea about what you want to manifest. When the energy of two equal and opposing ideas are given the same attention, you will naturally feel a conflict.

For instance, if you're saying on the one hand, "I really want to lose weight," and you're saying on the other hand, "I can't live or be happy unless I eat everything I want," you're going to be in a struggle, unable to fully commit. If you feel yourself wanting to become a new person, but experience resistance and struggle, let these feelings tell you that you are holding some concepts that will have to go because they are opposing your true intent of self-discovery. You will not need to fight with yourself to eliminate the self-concepts that stand in the way. But you will need to cling to the truth about yourself with focused commitment.

MOTIVATION

We have just discussed the role of constructive will power in the readiness stage of self-discovery. We have seen that when you're ready to discover your true self, your will is the engine that starts you and drives you through to the end. Your will is the force that gets you moving with a quality purpose and keeps you moving forward so that you don't give up. Now, what is the role of motivation at the readiness stage?

When you use your will to become willing, you can become highly motivated. This is the open state of mind you need to start your journey. Being willing allows you to be highly motivated because you don't set up ways to stop yourself before you start. To find out how motivated you really are, ask yourself, What obstacles am I willing to overcome to reach my goal? What am I willing to learn? How am I willing to change?

The third principle of mental conduct forms the foundation for your willingness: You have the ability to do, the capacity to act, and the capability to perform and produce. If you didn't have *ability, capacity,* and *capability,* you wouldn't have any motivation to change; whether or not you were willing to change wouldn't matter because you wouldn't have the ability. But since you do have these qualities, you must be willing to allow them to manifest, willing to encourage them to manifest. Here are some ways to do that.

Be Willing to Sacrifice a Worn-Out Self-Concept

You may say, "Of course, I'm willing to change. I want a new life. I want to become who I really am." You may feel highly motivated.

It's good that you say those words, but putting them into action requires letting go of old self-concepts that may be bound tightly to your personality. This is why I stress the inner power step of *sacrifice* as you get ready for self-discovery. Your willingness to change must be accompanied by a strong motivation to sacrifice certain aspects of yourself that are not truly you.

Just as you need to make your will pure and strong to start you on your path, your motivation must be pure and strong to help you from swerving from your path.

Usually there is an all-too-human tendency to give in to your past, unwanted self-concept even while you're trying to change it. When it comes time to let go of self-concepts like, "I'm an angry person," "I'm a worrier," "I'm a sad person," "I'm a sick person," "I'm a workaholic," or even, "I'm a doctor," "I'm a waiter," or whatever, this may feel like a supreme sacrifice. Since your present self is all you know, you may feel like the sacrifice of your undesirable traits, whatever they are, is a loss, not a gain. You may feel as if you're losing yourself.

Willing sacrifice is important in self-discovery, and difficult, because often you have to let go *before* you see the gain. You don't necessarily get to look before you leap into a new self-concept. There is a beautiful passage from the Bible:

> *When I was a child, I talked like a child, I thought like a child, I reasoned like a child. When I became a man, I put childish ways behind me. Now we see but a poor reflection as in a mirror; then we shall see face to face. Now I know in part; then I shall know in full, even as I am fully known.*
>
> I CORINTHIANS 13:11–12

It is not what we put on that tells us who we are; it is what we take off that lets us see who we already are. We see "but a poor reflection as in a mirror" when we look at ourselves through the mistakes, hurt, pain, guilt, and the opinions of others in the past. We see "face to face" when we become clear and transparent, and look within through the eyes of our Silent Master consciousness. Then we see and feel who we already are in truth *now*.

Your true self is already pure and true. When you sacrifice your negative traits, you clear the way to see who you really are.

Always Remember:
He Can Do, She Can Do, Why Not Me?

We've discussed how bad habits can feel like such a part of you that you begin to think that they *are* you. You must overcome this belief right at the start of the readiness stage, or you will be likely to sabotage your best efforts.

In my Jung SuWon teaching, I have a saying: He Can Do, She Can Do, Why Not Me? All your negative false beliefs can be changed because they do not reflect the true potential of your original self. Over and over again, my students have proved that they can do what seems impossible. After they enter a positive, supportive environment, they start to get in touch with the real and pure ideas of their true self. They begin to feel the power of the words *I can* and *I will* and *I know* that come from their Silent Master consciousness. Which is more difficult? Breaking ten bricks with your bare hands or asking your boss for a raise? For some, breaking ten bricks is easier.

One of my students weighed about three hundred pounds when she enrolled in my Jung SuWon classes. When it came time to do one of the exercises — a simple tumbling move, forward rolls on a mat — she quite naturally answered the question "Why Not Me?" with "Because I'm too fat!" To her surprise, she did it! What happened? She responded to the atmosphere of encouragement and accomplishment, and joined with others who were creating success. And this victory gave her confidence to go on and create more victories. As you might expect, she's doesn't weigh three hundred pounds anymore.

Being ready for change — ready for self-discovery — often means putting yourself in an environment that supports you. In this way, you are motivated by your environment instead of obstructed by it.

ATTITUDE

We have seen how your will power is like an engine that drives you along your path, and how motivation is like the fuel feeding the engine; think of attitude as that which determines the *quality* of the fuel. Positive attitudes are like high-energy fuel, such as high-octane gas. Negative attitudes are like impure gasoline. When you put impure gasoline into your car, you will undoubtedly see trouble in the engine before long. Just so, negative attitudes create obstruction and conflict in your life.

Attitudes are important at the start of your self-discovery process because they help determine the quality of your manifestations. Positive attitudes ensure that your will and motivation remain pure and powerful so that you create constructive forms in your life, forms that promote progress and acceleration and reflect the love, peace, and harmony of your true self.

Maintain a Receptive Attitude

One of the activities in our Self-Discovery Weekends is the Freedom Dance. In this exercise, I ask students to abandon themselves in joyful free-form movement around a fire for a symbolic shedding of the past. Because many people are unnecessarily critical of themselves (self-conscious), this dance is designed to foster the receptive attitude needed to pursue true self-discovery.

As mentioned in Chapter One, the willingness to be open and receptive to a new concept of your self and a new life is an attitude I call the empty cup. If you think you already know everything, if you think you already know yourself in total, your cup is already full and cannot hold anything new. This readiness — being open and receptive to a new direction — is a quality you need every day, not just once in your life when you decide to pursue your true self.

You may not feel uninhibited enough to do something like a freedom dance, even in the privacy of your own home, but here's something you can do every day to help create and maintain your empty cup: take a shower! Even if you don't have time to meditate, your shower can be a time for some valuable work for yourself. Since showering is an activity you usually do mindlessly, try doing it with thought and some enjoyable visualization.

Imagine that you're on a tropical island, and that your shower is actually a rushing waterfall surrounded by beautiful tropical flowers and birds. Gentle winds are blowing; a clear blue sky shows above. The falling water is clean, clear, sparkling with energy. As you stand there, the water flowing down on your body, you feel yourself open to receive the fresh, new energy in the water. Using your soap, you feel the falling water wash away your anxiety, your tension, your worries, your regrets, your frustrations. You feel the cleansing action washing away everything that clouds you or hurts you or limits you. You feel yourself becoming more and more free, more relaxed, more happy, more peaceful; the soap and sparkling water are washing away all your negativity. Let yourself believe the water and soap actually can do that for you. When the water goes down the drain, let yourself imagine that the ill-will, the hostility, the resentment, the anger, the stubbornness, the laziness, the jealousy — whatever — goes well away from you forever.

Do the same thing when you brush your teeth. As you rinse your mouth, let the water wash away the harsh words, the mistaken words, the words you may regret. When you wash your hair, let the shampoo wash away all the feelings and attitudes you've taken on that don't come from your true self, and cleanse all the actions you took that are now "on your head." What do you want to get out of your hair? As you dry yourself with the towel, think of your body and mind as now being new. This clean, new body is like a new sun rising on a new day. Yesterday is washed away.

When you do this shower meditation to eliminate negative thoughts and feelings, you are taking action to form an empty cup attitude. Remember, however, that to become empty does not mean that you become a void. In fact, the process of sacrificing your negative traits is best carried out through positive affirmation, not through negation. Instead of saying, "I am not sad," you say, "I am full of natural joy belonging to the consciousness of my Silent Master." Your empty cup will be filled by your positive declarations about your true self.

Maintain an Attitude of Anticipating Success

Since you co-create with the energy of thought and feeling, I say, have a large empty cup! Have unlimited thought about what you can accomplish. Have unlimited expectations for yourself.

When I say unlimited, I don't mean unreasonable. The fact is, your Silent Master will not give you unreasonable desires, but will give you your true desires. So, when I say that you should have unlimited expectations, I mean don't let anything limit the possibility of making your true desires come to life.

Somehow, as time goes by, we become impressed with the accomplishments of others, and conclude that we cannot express them ourselves. We usually find pretty good excuses why we can't, and continue to keep ourselves limited. "He

Can Do, She Can Do, Why Not Me?" In this saying is the encouragement to develop the attitude of always anticipating success. The arrow of this attitude takes you in the direction of accomplishment.

Realistic Expectations Turn into Goals

When you are willing to have reasonable expectations, setting goals is the next logical step to take. When you are willing to be receptive and open-minded, and when you have high expectations, you won't be afraid to set a goal, even if it presently seems out of reach.

In the readiness stage of self-discovery, what stands most in the way of setting goals is your concept of yourself. This is why it is so important to have an open mind when you set goals. Over and over, I hear people say things like, "I'm a very good organizer, but I'm not at all creative." Or, "I think I'm a pretty good mechanic, but I could never be a computer programmer." These comments demonstrate what I mean by holding a full cup. These people have sealed their fate with their limited beliefs. Often these comments are contradictions as well as being self-limiting. For example, the ability to bring organization into a state of confusion is not the opposite of creativity. Organizing is a highly creative process. How often we limit ourselves by how we define concepts!

Maintain a Forgiving Attitude

Once you have begun to set goals that go beyond your present concept of yourself, you may have to work hard at letting go of your past. A big part of the readiness phase of self-discovery is the elimination of the old to make room for the new. This may require much forgiveness on your part, because forgiveness is the way you release the past. You cannot change a situation if you keep holding onto it with negative emotion. You must forgive, release, and sacrifice feelings of condemnation in order to change any bad situation in your life.

Forgiving yourself is as important as forgiving others. You never need to condemn yourself or anyone else for mistakes. You simply learn whatever you need to learn from the mistake, let it go, and then move on to create a new reality.

Unfortunately, forgiveness can seem to demand the ultimate unwilling sacrifice. So much tempts us to hate and resent and be angry when we feel wronged. We don't easily sacrifice those feelings, and forgiveness almost seems to hurt when we're called upon to do it. But if you can do it, you find release, not loss. With forgiveness, you find freedom to create the new, unhindered by past impressions.

And perhaps what may be harder than forgiving others is forgiving yourself. The main obstacle to forgiving yourself is your feeling of guilt. If you think back to your childhood, you'll remember that condemnation was probably the most common way of dealing with wrongdoing. Most of us have been taught that when we did something wrong, we should be condemned before being forgiven, and maybe not even forgiven! Most of us were not taught that doing something wrong should be an opportunity for education, or an opportunity for creating a better solution.

Let Go of Self-Condemnation and Guilt

Most people are much too hard on themselves. When you see you've made a mistake, you don't have to pound yourself further into the ground. You need love — not condemnation, not punishment — when you recognize that you need to make a change. Self-condemnation and guilt prevent learning, because they keep you focused on what's wrong instead of on what's right. Condemnation and guilt form a negative emotional cloud that encourages and attracts more wrong-doing rather than healing.

One of the first steps to take in letting go of the past — and getting ready for a new life — is to realize that you don't need to feel guilty forever. Guilt has a purpose for a little while. It makes you realize you need to change. But once you take action to create change, guilt is no longer purposeful. In fact, at that point it's obstructive. So if you're ready to make a change right now, first let go of the guilt. Realize that your guilt is a feeling about something that's over. Whatever the "fault" or whatever the mistake, it isn't a part of the true you now. It's over. It's gone. Begin the process of healing with feelings of joy instead.

Here's a simple illustration that shows how forgiveness and letting go of condemnation or guilt bring healing.

Once there were two neighborhoods whose residents were constantly fighting. An argument between them had started many years before, and since that time they had always been at odds with each other.

Members from one neighborhood would not associate in any way with members from the opposite neighborhood. They had been separated for so long that nobody in one neighborhood knew anything about anybody in the other neighborhood.

One day, the people in one of the neighborhoods started having problems with their well. Slowly, they were losing their water. Everyone in that neighborhood tried to fix the problem, but it got worse. A few weeks later they were out of water completely. It looked like they would lose everything they had worked for — their farms, their cattle.

Finally, when the situation became desperate, their only option was to speak with the people in the other neighborhood about their problem. Swallowing their pride, they approached the other neighborhood. As they walked, visions of being ridiculed and rejected were in their minds, but their only hope was to try anyway.

The elders who had been part of the original dispute cautiously entered the hall where the elders of the other neighborhood were gathered. They explained their situation, and then waited anxiously as the council conferred.

To their amazement, the elders were sympathetic and compassionate. They volunteered their help and offered to share their well.

Together, the neighborhoods came to meet this challenge. They worked together to build canals and irrigation. Each discovered admirable qualities in the other, and grew so close in their endeavors that they became inseparable.

In somewhat the same way as the two neighborhoods, we have become separated from our true self, our Silent Master. We forget how and why we became so separated. In the story, this separation is symbolized by the well drying up. Sooner or later, however, some event usually turns us back to our Silent Master. Maybe it's an illness or failure that makes us seek our Silent Master again, or maybe it's a natural desire to simply know our real self. Whatever the reason, when we seek to find our real self, we may be filled with doubt and guilt, and we may feel undeserving or afraid to turn within for healing. But if we do, our Silent Master greets us with healing and love, not with rejection, just as the elders of the opposing neighborhood did And just as the two groups prospered greatly when they worked together, you can prosper with renewed power and strength when you join forces with your Silent Master. As the Silent Master image at the start of this chapter indicates, the immaterial aspect of yourself, your spiritual being, is intimately involved in the life you create, because matter and spirit exist at the same time.

Your Silent Master Consciousness knows Itself to be immaterial in substance, but It also takes form (manifests) as your physical body and the material world around you. Thus, you may describe yourself as being both immaterial (spiritual) and material (physical) at the same time.

This is why your Silent Master consciousness is so accessible to you. The return to your Silent Master consciousness is a return to an aspect of yourself that exists within you right now — right where you are.

CHOICE

At the start of your journey to self-discovery, you want to shake hands with your power of choice and love, and protect it forever. The person you are today is based on how you've chosen in the past to respond to your environment, to the people you've known, and to your own thoughts and feelings. The person you will be tomorrow is based on the choices you make regarding these same things right now. As long as you remain aware that your development depends on choices you make right now, you stay in the driver's seat to invite change and growth. But as long as you regard your present self as "just the way I am," as some sort of reality set in cement, you shut down the self-discovery process.

The fact is, you are as open as your choices are. You can choose to open and grow, you can choose one new goal after another, you can choose to abandon one way of life for another, you can choose to devote yourself to any reasonable pursuit. Or, you can choose to say "I can't." Your consciousness is standing behind your choices with the creative force to drive them into form.

If you are really ready to pursue a more unlimited concept of yourself, to explore your Silent Master consciousness, to become the creative driver of your life, then you are now ready to start exploring the tools and disciplines you will need along this path. In the next chapter we will do just that. We'll see that these tools and disciplines help you increase the energy you apply in creating your life.

What could be more worthy of your efforts than the discovery and fulfillment of your true being? I like the parable in the Bible that talks about the discovery of your real being:

> *The kingdom of heaven is like treasure hidden in a field. When a man found it, he hid it again, and then in his joy went and sold all he had and bought that field.... Again, the kingdom of heaven is like a merchant looking for fine pearls. When he found one of great value, he went away and sold everything he had and bought it.*
>
> MATTHEW, 13:44–45

Your Silent Master consciousness is like the pearl of great value for which you will sell all to possess, because when you possess the consciousness that *is* the source of all, you likewise possess all. Isn't it worth your time and effort to discover this powerful aspect of your consciousness and begin to use it constructively?

PRACTICE

In the readiness phase of self-discovery, it's important to think about exactly what you'd like to discover in yourself. The following questions can help you analyze your present self in a general way, and in so doing, help you get ready to form some new self-concepts. Write out your answers, or at least think through your answers slowly and thoroughly.

1. What does self-discovery mean to you now? Or, put another way, what would you like self-discovery to accomplish for you?

2. What is happening in your life now that you want to change, improve, accelerate, and so on?

3. What methods or strategies have you already used to accomplish the goals you named in the second question, and how well have they worked?

4. What are ten different adjectives that describe your personality? Be sure to include both positive and negative traits.

5. What are the three happiest times you've experienced in your life? The three saddest? The three angriest?

6. What long-term goals have you set?

7. Do you have some goals you would like to set but feel out of reach or impossible?

MEDITATION

Right now my Silent Master consciousness is pure, perfect, whole, and complete. Every idea that I am, exists right now, right here. Right now, I am open to see the pure and perfect expression of all ideas in my Silent Master consciousness. I am open to see all the people, circumstances, and events in my life cooperating with each other harmoniously and expressing love. All the ideas in my Silent Master consciousness already exist in peaceful cooperation, harmony, and love, and I am open to see and feel these ideas in me. Therefore, I am willing to release the limited and negative pictures I see with forgiveness, and strive to create love, peace, joy, harmony, and unity wherever I am. I accept my responsibility as co-creator of this world with joy and love.

CHAPTER THREE

ENERGIZING:
BUILDING CREATIVE POWER

SILENT MASTER IMAGE IV

YOU ARE CREATIVE ENERGY

Your Silent Master knows Itself as the Source of mental, emotional, and material Energy — your Energy, which you are free to utilize and control in creating what you desire. Therefore, you are a Co-Creator, cooperating with the Life Force of the Universe to shape yourself and the world around you.

In the previous chapter we looked at the ways we become ready to discover our true self. We discussed the importance of harnessing the power of our will, of strong motivation, and of constructive attitudes. We must now mobilize all our energy to stand behind this commitment! And this means we'll focus on the inner power we possess to correctly utilize our energy.

We are going to explore energy in this chapter — what it is, and how to use it. We do not generally understand how we sabotage our goals and efforts by misusing our own energy. When we understand what our energy is and what it can do, we become highly motivated to purify our energy in order to increase it.

WHAT IS INCREASED ENERGY?

An important universal law of physics states that energy cannot be created or destroyed. It can only change from one form to another. Light can change to heat, for example; heat can turn into mechanical work; love can manifest into friends cooperating in harmony. All the energy in the universe already exists (it does not increase), and is available to you right now. So when we talk about increasing your energy, we are really talking about how you can make more of your natural energy more accessible to you. You can learn to purify your energy so that you create greater freedom and happiness.

Where do you find this energy? As the Silent Master Image at the start of this chapter indicates, your Silent Master consciousness within you now is "the Source of mental, emotional, and material Energy — your Energy, which you are free to utilize and control in creating what you desire." All the energy in the universe is already here now — at one with you — ready to be transformed by you. To increase your energy, you need to remove what stands in the way of experiencing the pure force and pure Love of your Silent Master. As you discover your true self, you experience more of your true energy. This energy never actually increases, but because you remove the obstacles to your pure energy, you experience *more* of it.

What, then, stands in the way of experiencing all the beautiful energy of your Silent Master? If we want to go directly to the energy of our Silent Master, where do we go? Where do we find It? As Silent Master Image I says in Chapter One, "It expresses Itself through your thinking, through true Ideas and Thoughts in your mind." So, pure energy is expressed through your thinking.

And as Silent Master Image III says in Chapter Two, ". . . It also takes form (manifests) as your physical body and material world around you." So, pure energy is expressed through your body and through the material world.

Since the energy of our Silent Master can be expressed through our thinking and through our material world, to feel Its pure and powerful energy we have to cut through, and cut out, all the obstructive aspects of our thinking and our environment.

How do we do that? We do it through a process I call *energizing*. The process of energizing involves using specific tools and techniques to peel away layers of obstruction and limitation in our thinking and in our environment so that we feel the natural energy that already exists. To get more energy, you don't just turn the water faucet to open it wider. In your original energy state, the "faucet" is already turned on and open wide. Our job is to get the rocks out of the pipe so that the water — our natural energy — flows without obstruction. Removing the "rocks" is the purification process, so I stress the inner power step of purity in the energizing stage of self-discovery. In short, receiving more energy comes from being more aware of your true self. Energizing is what you do to eliminate limited self-concepts so that you become your true self.

Why do you want to feel more of your natural energy? Because it gives you feelings of freedom and joy and love and creativity. These qualities make life worth living! Your energy is naturally creative. We could say it *wants* to take form, just as all the material energy in the universe constantly changes form. You may have misused your energy in ways that make your life limited and unhappy. With self-discovery, you will use energy in ways that make you more free and happy.

Discover the energy of your original self! We will examine energy, look at the ways in which it manifests, and see how you can purify yourself to receive more of your original, natural energy and to use it creatively.

INVISIBLE ENERGY
CREATES VISIBLE MANIFESTATIONS

When you look at the world you see different kinds of energy in motion. Energy is essentially an invisible force; the only way we know it exists is the way we see it manifest. We see electrical energy manifest by using our appliances and machines; we see nature's energy manifest as it pushes grass and trees out of the ground, as it creates blowing winds and storms; we see solar energy manifest by its quiet, steadfast, radiant light and warmth; we see physical energy manifest as human bodies that walk, talk, work, and play, and as animals run and hunt. Finally, we see biological energy, the force which manifests as life. Let's start here: with life.

THE ORIGINAL LIFE FORCE
CREATES ALL MANIFESTATION

Life exists all by itself. We do not create life. Only Life can create life. The Life Force of the universe is the creative force that brings everything into existence. Your Silent Master is connected with this Life Force, which is why you are here and alive.

Life, then, is energy. It is the energy that makes your heart beat and makes you breathe, that causes the cells of your body to automatically grow and reproduce the moment you are conceived.

Life energy is spiritual energy. Yes, we see it here in this dimension as a material, physical manifestation. But the real energy behind this physical manifestation — driving it, creating it, sustaining it — is spiritual.

So we can say that the life force is a manifestation force. And here's the way it works: When you mentally conceive, you set the creative process in motion. What you conceive in consciousness provides energy to encourage a manifestation to take form. That's because what you conceive — or perceive — is the starting point for all your decisions, actions, responses, judgments, and attitudes. These things directly or indirectly help create your self-concept, your body, and the environment around you.

As Silent Master Image IV says at the beginning of this chapter: ". . . You are a Co-Creator, cooperating with the Life Force of the Universe to shape yourself and the world around you." How do you cooperate with the Life Force? By correctly utilizing the energy of the Life Force, expressed through your thinking, your body, and your material world.

IDEAS ARE THE ORIGINAL LIFE FORCE, THE ORIGINAL CREATIVE ENERGY

Manifestations of all things reside in your Silent Master consciousness as ideas. The ideas then respond to the creative life force in your Silent Master consciousness, and manifest in this dimension as different material shapes and forms.

And where do your manifestations take place? Out there in the world, you may say. But where is the world? Doesn't the manifestation of the world take place in your own sensing of it? Aren't all your senses of taste, touch, smell, vision, and hearing in your consciousness? Everything you know about yourself in the world appears in something we can call your mentality. You may argue that you're also physical — not only mental. But you know about your physicalness because your awareness of it is processed through your mind.

Again, as Silent Master Image IV says: "Your Silent Master knows Itself as the Source of mental, emotional, and material Energy . . . which you are free to utilize and control. . . ."

Ideas Are Eternal and Real; Manifestations Are Temporary and Unreal

Here's another truth about manifestations: They don't last. Isn't it true that both you and, say, a car, will "die" or disintegrate after something called time takes place? This brings us to another question: What is death? If everything is energy, what happens to that energy in death? After all, doesn't the universal law of conservation of energy state that energy cannot be created or destroyed? Of course, we know our material forms turn to dust and are recycled back to molecules and atoms that merge with the air and earth. In that sense, our material energy is transformed, not destroyed. But the question remains: Why do we perceive death? To answer that, we have to discuss the difference between real and unreal.

The Difference Between Real and Unreal

Here's a truth about your Silent Master consciousness: It is eternal. Although this seems ironic, our perception of death and the disintegration of all forms in the world are possible only because the ideas in the Silent Master consciousness are eternal.

Does that sound like a contradiction? Let me explain further. In reality, there is no death. All that seems to be born and die is the coming and going of some manifestation of some idea in your Silent Master consciousness. You may ask, "But if something comes and goes, isn't that death? How can you say there's no death when someone or something goes away?"

Here's where the difference between real and unreal becomes important. The only thing that "dies" is something unreal. All things that die in the material world are not real in the same way that the ideas of your Silent Master are real. Since ideas cannot be destroyed, we say they are real. The forms that are created from ideas are unreal because they can be destroyed.

That which can't be destroyed is real. That which can be destroyed is unreal.

For example, I can think of the idea of "beauty" quite easily. I can think of beauty whether I'm here on earth or in space because beauty exists everywhere. When I die, beauty will still be in the world. No one can destroy it. Beauty is eternal and can't be destroyed because it exists as an idea in consciousness. That is the nature of any idea in consciousness: It is eternal.

However, if I make a beautiful object, such as a red velvet chair, beauty is no longer just an idea, but has manifested materially as a beautiful piece of furniture. The chair, unlike the idea behind it, is automatically limited; that is the nature of a manifestation. Unlike the unlimited, eternal idea of beauty that preceded the chair, the chair is local and exists in only a few feet of space. If the chair catches fire, this particular manifestation of beauty will "die," but the idea of beauty will still be alive.

Beauty — like all other ideas in the Silent Master consciousness such as love, harmony, peace, unity — is also *infinite*. That is, beauty can manifest in an infinite number of ways, and have an infinite number of forms. Right now, where you sit, look around and see in how many places and in how many ways the idea of beauty is manifested. Right now, looking out into my garden, I see beautiful plants. I see beauty in my home, I see beauty in the eyes of the people I know, in works of art, in the movement of dancers. The idea of beauty is all around you in many different forms. These forms will disappear some time, but the idea of beauty will never pass away.

The ideas within you are the real things in life. When one of the prisoners of war was released after the war with Iraq, he made some interesting comments about "reality." He said that when he was captured and life was possibly going to be taken from him, he didn't think at all about the material aspects of his life that he might lose — career, money, houses, stocks, or cars — which he thought he had valued. Instead, his thoughts turned naturally to real things — the love of his family, the sharing and caring he had known with his wife and children. He turned to the eternal ideas, the things that survive after all else turns to dust.

Ideas Are Creative Energy

Although we have material goals, our first goal is to become aware of the real and eternal qualities and ideas that stand behind the creation of our material goals. Why? Because if you focus your energy only on material forms, you limit yourself to energy that is ultimately unreal and possibly faulty.

For example, let's say you want to launch a new, satisfying career. There is nothing wrong with this goal, but there would be something wrong if you decided that only one specific job in one particular company down the street would meet your needs. If you focused all your energy on winning that job in that location, you would set yourself up for possible failure, disappointment, and resentment when it didn't happen. Instead, focus your energy on developing the ideas and qualities necessary for the work you want, such as self-esteem, proper training, specific skills, and perseverance. Thus prepared, you would have the power to obtain an appropriate job in any number of companies. Even if you lost your job in one company, you would still have at your disposal the same ideas and qualifications to help you create a similar kind of position elsewhere.

Similarly, if you want love in your life, it's not effective to focus your energy on a particular person and decide that particular person is the only one who can meet your needs. Rather, focus your energy on the *idea* of love, expressing love and receiving love in many different ways. Then the appropriate persons will find their way to you.

When you discover the energy of your true self, your Silent Master consciousness, you'll find it contains the ideas that stand behind everything you desire to co-create. Because your ideas are eternal and infinite, you are an unlimited being, full of unlimited potential to manifest. This energy aspect of you is eternal and undying.

Your life right now is a picture of the ideas you presently hold. If you don't like the picture you have created of your life, you will have to let go of the particular consciousness energy that helped to create the undesirable forms, and reach for the pure consciousness energy of your Silent Master within.

The ideas in your Silent Master consciousness are pure and perfect, so when you want to change your life, seek those pure ideas first.

TWO ENERGY TOOLS:
THOUGHT AND EMOTION

There are two basic inner tools to use to discover your true self and change your life: thought and emotion.

When something in your life starts to go wrong, you will probably discover that your thoughts and feelings are contributing to the problem. For example, suppose a person finds that his normally successful business suddenly starts failing. Perhaps he finds his employees have become reckless and unreliable, he fails to collect payment for services from clients, and he finds that certain of his vendors are dishonest. Perhaps his first tendency is to think of himself as a victim, and to blame and criticize everyone around him for the trouble. But soon he discovers that this kind of thinking doesn't correct the situation. Then, still thinking that the problem is entirely outside of him, he attempts to correct the situation by firing certain employees and suing his clients for payment. Still he finds that his problems persist.

It probably is not readily apparent to this person that his failure may have formed as a result of an emotional pattern such as a fear of success. His business may have prospered initially because of his good desire and intent to form a successful business; in fact, his good intent may have been the very thing that hid his fear from his awareness. But because he is afraid of success, he unconsciously surrounds himself with people who will help to create a picture of failure — after all, he's the one who selected the vendors and hired the inadequate employees. His fear is carefully hidden, however, like most fears, and it doesn't occur to him to look within for the source of the trouble. He also may not be educated to see the connection between our emotional patterns and the actions we take.

Striving for emotional purity, then, is a valuable tool in the creation of your goals. If you are unaware of your emotional patterns, look at the pictures of your life. What do the pictures of your environment and relationships look like? Do you see lack of space, confinement, discord, disagreement, lack of unity, failure, repeating patterns of conflict? Be willing to acknowledge that there may be a connection between your fears, weaknesses, expectations (or lack of expectations) and the pictures that you see. Be willing to become aware of your fears, because an emotional pattern such as a fear of success will go on creating one picture of failure after another until it is corrected.

We do not always readily turn within to find the source of our problems. Yet that is what we must learn to do if we wish to bring about lasting change in our lives. You can always seek professional help to aid you in identifying and changing mental or emotional patterns. Meditation, which we will discuss shortly, is another way of turning within to look for answers and solutions. Your Silent Master is ready to help you as well. Your Silent Master consciousness is your true self, so It knows what patterns you are holding that obstruct and limit you. When you need an answer to a problem that is beyond your immediate knowing, you can turn to your Silent Master for guidance and awareness.

MENTAL, EMOTIONAL, AND PHYSICAL DISCIPLINES SPEED YOUR PROGRESS

Since like the businessman just mentioned, we create what we are, we need to purify our mental and emotional energy to manifest optimum power and perfection in our life.

Remember, one of the seven steps to self-discovery and inner power is to live out the principle that body and mind are one. Whatever happens in your mind happens next in your body or material world. Bear this principle in mind as we discuss another one of the seven steps to inner power, that of purity. We will look at ways to purify your body, mind, and emotions so that the pure energy of your Silent Master consciousness shines forth, creating a new and truer life for you.

Your mind is the environment in which your ideas, thoughts, and emotions reside. As with any environment, the goal is to make it as clean and pure as possible. I often find that people treat their cars better than they treat their minds and bodies. Their cars at least get regular tune-ups, good gas, careful washing and cleaning. But the content and quality of their minds — their thoughts and feelings — don't get any attention at all!

Since your Silent Master consciousness is perfect purity, you don't need to work to make yourself pure. You need to work to eliminate the thoughts and emotions that are impure from your mind and environment. You will be taking away what isn't you in order to leave what is you shining forth.

How will you do this? Two very important mental tools to use are *concentration* and *visualization*. We will study these concepts, as well as other ways you can purify your mental and emotional energy.

Concentration Focuses Energy

Both concentration and visualization are forms of meditation. Both promote purity because they require that you narrow your focus. Why narrow your focus? Because a sharp, narrow focus helps you separate what you don't want from what you do want.

The basic rule is this: Whatever you concentrate on and visualize, you propel into manifestation. As we have said, your thoughts are creative energy. Concentration and visualization are ways of using this consciousness to focus on and energize a desired goal.

Concentration means that you will mentally focus on something — an idea, a feeling, a concept — and eliminate everything else from your mental environment. Concentration does not come easily to the modern mind, which has been overstimulated by the constant, aggressive sights and sounds of the media. Television alone has done a lot to turn us into couch potatoes, to teach us to be passive victims of outside stimulation. You must become able to shut out outside stimulation and turn within. It takes full attention to concentrate properly, and you may have to train yourself before you can do it well.

Concentration requires quietude, perseverance, and self-control. It is a process that can be carried out in formal meditation, and is also a process that you carry out every day in all kinds of little ways. (This is covered in Chapter Six.)

Concentration is a discipline. As you discipline your mind through concentration, your mind becomes that of a student. You help your mind learn to focus only on what you desire to create, not to bubble and cook in a stew of unwanted, self-destructive thoughts.

Here is a simple meditation process you can do to test or develop your powers of concentration:

1. Sit with your legs crossed and your hands at your side or in your lap.

2. For a few minutes, time your breathing so that you inhale for a count of six and exhale for a count of six. This is, in itself, a form of concentration, and as a result your breathing will automatically slow down. As your breathing slows, inhale and exhale for longer counts.

3. When you feel calm and relaxed, take your mind off your breathing and allow yourself to breathe normally as your body desires.

4. Choose a thought you wish to propel into manifestation, such as, *The solution to this problem is here now and appears to me in the right way at the right time,* or *I have all the money I need to abundantly meet my expenses.* As you mentally say these words, allow a feeling of peace and acceptance to energize the concept. Even though the concept hasn't taken form yet, describe the finished form of that desire and don't worry about how the details of getting there will manifest. You may find you can slip back and forth between the words and the feeling that accompanies your words, focusing on one or the other without losing the concept.

5. As you concentrate, you will probably notice that additional thoughts break in — sometimes aggressively — and you may even find at some point that you have abandoned your concept altogether. This is the undisciplined mind in action. It can be really clever in taking you away from your concentration and sending you running down another track.

6. When you find additional thoughts breaking in, or if you find you have abandoned your concentration, do not resist or fight. Let go of the new thoughts and quietly, but firmly, return to the focus of your concentration. As you continue to do this, eventually your mind "learns" not to interrupt your concentration. But you may need considerable practice periods to gain the mastery you desire.

Always state your concentrations in positive terms. Never concentrate on something like "I am not poor"; say instead, "I am abundantly supplied." When you state things in the negative, you're actually concentrating on the negative!

You can do a similar type of concentration throughout your day by deciding to catch yourself in negative thinking and replace the negative thoughts with some kind of positive affirmation. This is particularly useful, for instance, when you are trying to heal a physical condition. Your concentration throughout the day may be to deliberately turn your thoughts away from the pain (or away from the appearance) every time it enters your mind. Such a discipline does wonders to eliminate something that has gained momentum in your life solely because of your attention to it.

You can also do the same type of meditation described above without concentrating on anything in particular. Your simple intent of wanting to open to the awareness of your Silent Master and to experience Its light, peace, and silence is a refreshing and energizing meditation.

Visualization Captures the Energy of Ideas

As we discussed, material forms are pictures of our ideas in consciousness. Remember that everything you see existed first as an idea that you entertained. When you want to change the picture, then, you must work with the ideas, not only with the picture.

Imagine you're looking at a picture of a 35mm slide projected on a screen. What you see on the screen comes from the slide in the projector. Any markings you make on the screen to change the picture will not change the picture on the slide. The slides in the projector are like ideas in consciousness. Just as you must change the slide to change the picture on the screen, you must change your ideas, attitudes, and expectations to change the picture of your world.

When you want a particular manifestation to take place, you may not know exactly how to frame your thinking so that you focus on the right ideas. This is where visualization can help you. Since the visible form is a picture of your ideas, holding the picture in mind automatically connects you to the idea attached to the picture. Visualizing the picture of the desired manifestation will help propel it into form.

Since pictures are connected to ideas, they have energy just as ideas do. The energy in your mental pictures is what encourages them to manifest materially. Because mental pictures have creative energy, you must be careful what you entertain in your mind's eye. How much of your time do you spend visualizing past events that you want to eliminate? We have a tendency to dwell on the issues we dislike, often visualizing and rehearsing them with great passion and intensity. This activity only keeps the undesired energy "alive," and works against the energy of any other positive images we may strive to create.

Just as you purify your thinking by choosing what thoughts and words you will concentrate on, you must purify the images you visualize. You can use the meditation we just used for concentrating on an idea for your visualization. Instead of dwelling on the words that describe an idea you want to manifest, dwell on the picture of your desired manifestation. During that time, allow no other pictures to enter your mind.

You may find visualization difficult: Just as extraneous thoughts try to crowd out the focus of your concentration, many other pictures and images may intrude on your visualization. Without resisting or wrestling with the distraction, gently return to your visualization every time you catch yourself wandering. Soon your mind will obediently learn that you won't accept intrusions. Of course, there's nothing wrong with using both words and pictures in your visualization.

Candle Meditation

Here is a visual meditation I use to open my awareness to my spiritual self. The candle, and special rituals with fire or light, have been used for this purpose for thousands of years. Light has special mystical significance to our inner being. It's not by accident that candles are lighted to show respect at special occasions or extraordinary events, or to show honor for revered persons, or to deliver a special message as protesters do when they hold lighted candles in a march, or to add significance to religious ceremonies. Intuitively, we know our inner being is light, and the candle helps us turn our attention to our spiritual being, especially when we need help above and beyond our material efforts. The flame reminds us of our pure being — the clarity, warmth, life, and love that burns in our Silent Master consciousness.

In the biblical account of creation, for instance, the first command of creation is "Let there be light: and there was light." The first and purest form of material manifestation is *light*.

Likewise, the first and purest material manifestation of your Silent Master consciousness is light. Light is the link between who you are as pure consciousness and who you are as matter. Pure light is unformed and unshaped like pure consciousness, yet it is the medium that shapes and forms itself into material manifestation. It is the link between the formed and the unformed. The candle meditation connects you with this aspect of yourself — energizing this inner aspect of your being by focusing on it.

In a quiet place where you can be alone, light a candle. As the light burns, allow yourself to feel blended with the flame, consciously knowing that as your perception unites with the flame, you simultaneously become one with the light of your inner being. This act of lighting the candle is like the beginning of creation. You are saying, "Let there be light in my life." You allow your mind to focus only on the flame in order to quiet your mind, and to still any restless thoughts and feelings that may try to distract you. The more your mind becomes still, calm, and undistracted, the more you become open to receiving the beautiful, clear impressions of your Silent Master.

Take as much or as little time with this meditation as you wish.

Physical Discipline Helps Energize You

Some people say, "I don't have time to worry about physical exercise right now. I have other problems. All I want to do is just get my life together at this point."

As I've said before, body and mind are one. Because your body is connected with your mind, bringing your body under control means bringing your mind under control. And vice versa, of course. Whatever disciplines you apply to your mind affect your body.

Since your body and mind are connected, you can use physical exercise to help purify your mind. Remember, when you purify your mind and body, you increase your energy. And you purify your mind and body by doing everything you can to remove limitation. Because body and mind are one, when you overcome physical limitation, you simultaneously overcome mental limitation.

It's a two-way process. For instance, when you encourage your body to go the extra mile around the track, one more mile than you did the day before, you're sending a message to your mind that says, "I can grow; I can change; I can break limits." This good message that your mind receives when you demand extra performance from your body then goes on to encourage even better performance, and not just in running. The message will now extend to other areas of your life. "I can grow; I can change; I can break limits" could also help you create new and better procedures at work that result in a promotion or a better position.

Your Body Deserves Respect

Your body is the most elegant creation you possess. Your body is the *embodiment* of ideas in your Silent Master consciousness. Just as you learn to use your mind properly, think of how important it is, then, to use and care for your body with the same respect and holiness you accord your spiritual consciousness. How? Just as you properly use and exercise your thought, so you should properly use and exercise your body. You've begun to learn that there is much more you can do with your mind; don't you think there is much more you can do with your body?

Discipline of the body works to discipline the mind. Discipline your mind and you strengthen your body.

Appreciation is the first step. What if you could use only certain parts of your body? Have you ever thought of what you would do if you had only one arm? Or no arms? Or no sight? Most people who enter my martial arts school are physically healthy and take their bodies for granted. It's for this reason I sometimes have them try to do what they think are normal everyday things without the use of their legs or arms or eyes. Very quickly they learn how complex the movements of their hands can be, or how precious their sight is. Your body is a miraculous gift. Utilize it, care for it, strengthen it. Don't waste it or take it for granted.

Food is also created from consciousness, as everything else is. Since your body is the temple of your Silent Master consciousness, give it the loving food and exercise that expresses your intent to be pure, real, and whole.

Eating Is an Energy Exchange

When you prepare and eat food, you are harnessing the energy in the vegetables, grains, or meats to interact with your energy, thereby creating more energy. Naturally you always want to eat the best quality food you can. But some people ask me what to do when they're traveling and have to eat junk food at times. Because food exists in consciousness, it has the energy of consciousness. When you eat, you bring this energy into your body. If you're in a situation where junk food is your only choice, remember that your positive attitude helps you get the best energy you can out of the food until a better selection is available.

It's your attitude toward what you eat — no matter whether it's vegetables or hot dogs — that is the most important thing. Of course, vegetables and hot dogs have different nutritional value. Choose the purest, highest quality food you can in the circumstances.

The energy in foods is not all the same. Apples grown in an environment of greed, commercialism, and neglect will not have the same energy as apples grown in an orchard where the farmer lovingly attended the trees, bestowed the best of plant foods and soil, and eliminated poisons from the environment. The consciousness involved in the creation of the apples is different in each case.

Likewise, when you prepare your food, the energy you put into the process will affect the quality of the outcome. Was your food prepared with love and care and the will to nourish? Or was it prepared with feelings of anger and resentment, anxiety and hurry? When you eat food prepared either way, it will have a nourishing quality that corresponds to the energy and intent of the preparer.

Breathing Is Energy in Action

Just as eating is the manifestation of an idea in consciousness, so is breathing. Breathing is the material way you exercise your connection to the life force of your Silent Master
consciousness. When you draw in air and exhale, it is also
how you take in the life force of your true self; you can take in
this life force because you are connected to it, just as your
physical breathing is "connected" to the atmosphere.

Breathing exercises can be a powerful tool in the energizing process because they help connect you with your life
force. You may have noticed that breathing is used by many
different doctors and therapists to help hurt, anxious, or
shocked patients regain control of themselves.

When you consciously connect with your breathing, you
consciously connect with your life force. Your breathing
directly connects you to your inner power. When you take
control of your breathing, you take control of your inner
power in a general way. That's why women in childbirth
classes learn breathing techniques to help them control the
process and dissipate pain.

Your body processes, your thoughts, and emotions all
respond to changes in your breathing. Thus, you can alter
your mental and emotional state by altering your breathing.
Have you noticed that when you're deep in thought, focused,
concentrating intensely on something, your breathing is
deep and slow? When you are anxious and excited your
breathing is shallow and fast paced. When you're shocked,
frightened, or extremely angry, your breathing may actually
stop momentarily. But if you deliberately take control of
your breathing and slow it down, your mental or emotional
state will start to calm down. That's why I ask you to start
your formal meditations by deliberately slowing your breathing. In this way, you're taking control of your mind and

encouraging it to form the calm, focused, receptive state necessary to begin the meditation.

Physical Exercise Is Energy in Motion

If you want greater physical freedom, you must understand that your body will respond very much to your mind, and your mind will respond to what you do with your body. Free physical movement is a picture of the free mobility of consciousness. Have you tried to play a good game of your favorite sport when your mind was preoccupied with a worrisome situation? You may have noticed that when you're tense and nervous, your body doesn't move freely and easily. The tense state literally tends to keep your muscles rigid. And just the reverse is true: When you are happy and relaxed, your physical movement is generally free and easy.

Even the medical profession recognizes the connection of body and mind in the physical therapy process. A person who must learn to walk again after an accident goes through many emotional and mental changes in the process of reconnecting with the walking muscles. Therapists work with the patients' attitudes as well as with their muscle groups.

Let your body help you develop better mental concepts. Since your body is connected to consciousness, watch your physical states and see what they may be telling you about your thinking. Your body shows you — in one way or another — your mental state. Depressed people slouch and shuffle. Happy people have a bounce and lightness in their step. When your body is acting tired and sluggish and you know you're healthy and have had plenty of rest, what is your body telling you? What is it you don't want to do? What are you "too tired" to confront or overcome? What are you "sick and tired" of?

Your health also mirrors the quality of your mental state. Have you noticed that the symptoms of colds and crying are similar? Isn't it true that the sniffles, the watery eyes, the hoarse voice, the tight, painful chest and draggy body are the same when you have a cold and when you're sad, and you hurt, and you cry? When you're chronically depressed, your immune system doesn't function as well in protecting you from viruses So when you have a cold, see if there is actually some emotional pain you haven't confronted behind your depressed immune system. You may be surprised how much faster the cold dissipates when you deal with the mental pain and your immune system snaps back.

Even if you are not a "physical" person — *especially* if you are not a physical person — try demanding more physical action from yourself. Let this demand send a message to your mind that you want to be more free and more unlimited, whether that means getting some kind of healing, or gaining more stamina, or simply expanding your concept of yourself.

When you push yourself physically and make demands on yourself for greater physical freedom, you can't help but grow spiritually. You are insisting that the freedom of your original self manifest physically and materially. This is why physical training is an important part of the Jung SuWon training I teach. By disciplining the body into accepting more power and more ability to perform, your mind responds with more power and more ability to perform. This interplay is energizing. The more limitation you overcome, the more of your natural energy you can experience.

Any kind of physical training you undertake will help to develop your physical freedom. It doesn't have to be a martial art. As part of your spiritual journey, then, allow a physical discipline to become part of your life. Body and mind are one; as you develop one, you develop the other. Not every-one's physical capabilities are the same. Ballet training may be right for one person, but the physical aspect of gardening may be a better choice and challenge for another.

INTERACTING WITH ENERGY FIELDS

Energy has a characteristic of being dynamic — that is, it doesn't stay put. All you have to do is study electrical energy to see how energy fields move around — attracting, repelling, moving, and interacting. Your own energy does the same.

Just as you put energy into your food when you grow it or prepare it, you also fill your environment with your energy. A room full of people creates an energy field that can be positive or negative, depending on everyone's intent. Is the intent to harmonize and cooperate? Or is the intent for many different wills to each have their way? We've all had the experience in families or other groups where the results of either kind of field — oppression or joy — can be felt.

The pure ideas and feelings of the Silent Master consciousness are of a higher energetic level than negative ideas and emotions. Love is a higher energy than hate; generosity is a higher energy than greed; unity is a higher energy than conflict; harmony is a higher energy than discord. All of these energy states can exist in consciousness, but a higher energy state has the effect of canceling out a lower energy state.

The Best Defense Is the High Energy of Love

According to the laws of electricity, electrical energy flows from a positive state to a negative. Your energy behaves like electrical energy. So, if you are manifesting a high positive energy state and come in contact with a lower negative energy state, energy naturally moves from the higher to the lower, not vice versa. This means that when you are manifesting a high, positive energy state and you come into the presence of a low energy state (like a lot of negative or angry people), one of two things will happen. One is that the negative energy can drain you. You might begin to feel tired and become negative as well. But, on the other hand, if you use your will and positive attitude to maintain your high state, you will cancel the negative state instead. This is the power of Love. When you consciously love, you create a field that can't hold ill will, harm, or hurt. Love is the greatest protection of all.

How do you keep your love in a negative environment? You let yourself be aware of the negativity, because ignoring it would be a form of acceptance and you might be drained. You then refuse to react emotionally to the negativity, because by reacting negatively you add your energy to it. Simply focus on your positive state, affirming that the reality of your mental state has the power to cancel or transform a lower negative state. This is all done quietly within your consciousness. Your presence does all the work. Why? Because your presence is the positive field created by the love you hold in your consciousness.

One person in a true loving state of mind can walk into a room full of angry people and create calm within a matter of minutes. You, then, are the creator of harmony or disharmony in your relationships according to how you supervise your own consciousness.

Your Environment Is a Picture of Your Self-Concept

People tend to seek out environments where there is energy similar to their own. People who gather together and stay together tend to have the same kind of energy level.

You've probably noticed that groups give approval to the individual members of the group, and this encourages the members to stay on that energy level. For instance, if you're in a group that likes to gossip about others, you will be accepted and supported if you join in. Sometimes groups exert pressure for good causes. The point is, you want to *choose* what group you will or won't belong to so you stay in control of your energy. You don't want to be a victim of group pressure.

When you are trying to purify your energy, be very aware of where you mingle, not because you are afraid of any environment, but simply because you wish to direct your energy in a particular way. One of my students, for example, went back to a place where he had lived before studying Jung SuWon for several years. While he was there, he went to one of the old bars where he used to hang out. When he walked in, he was amazed that he had ever spent time there. The place was dark and had a terrible smell, and the noise was loud and obnoxious. His first reaction was to walk out again. He had changed so much that the place felt alien and unpleasant. But he saw some people he knew, and decided he would stay long enough to be friendly. He said that it was only a matter of ten minutes before he stopped minding the darkness, the smell, or the noise. Everything that had been so unpleasant a few minutes before began to smoothly melt away.

This story shows what I mean about your high energy being drained away if you don't consciously prevent it. To prevent setbacks, avoid being over-confident when you start to make progress in increasing your energy. Self-confidence is an important part of expressing your energy positively and constructively, but you must never be so confident that you let down your guard unwisely. This student relaxed his state of mind because he wasn't aware how fast energy can be brought down without a lot of guarding, and it caused him to sink to a lower state. He learned a great lesson from this experience, and realized he had more work to do in protecting a pure state of mind.

As you go down the path of true self-discovery, your Silent Master consciousness will give you direction regarding where to direct your energy and how to purify it. You will find yourself leaning naturally toward certain kinds of food, desiring certain types of exercise, and inclining toward specific activities. These desires will feel quite compelling sometimes, a feeling that you positively *must* do a particular thing. But you will also have a feeling of peace and harmony about the direction you take.

Be willing to change direction at any time to respond to the guidance of the Love energy within you. This listening will be an important aspect of the life examination process, which we discuss in the next chapter.

PRACTICE

ONE

As you purify your energy, it's important to recognize the positive qualities you already demonstrate. Split yourself in two for a moment, and list the positive and negative qualities you possess. Don't be surprised if you have to work hard at this, especially at acknowledging your good nature. In order to control and purify your energy, you have to know where you stand first! Since you may not be used to observing yourself, this will be a good practice to find out how to direct your efforts. Try it like this:

Desirable Qualities
I make an effort to eat pure, balanced foods.

Undesirable Qualities
I get angry at slight provocation and usually cause a fight.

TWO

Practice identifying the attitudes and conditions that affect your energy. Events in your life are teachers and give you much feedback about what works and what doesn't. Think about your past and ask what specifically happened here or there that played a role in creating constructive changes for you. Think of a situation in which your energy changed in a significant way. What did you do to change your energy? What happened as a result? You can probably find instances when certain negative attitudes or actions created a negative result, and instances when either consciously or by accident you took an action that worked positively for you.

MEDITATION

Right now, my Silent Master is the energy behind everything I experience. My Silent Master is Love, and everywhere I look, I see the opportunity to discover the presence of love. My Silent Master is Truth, so everywhere I go, I can put my truth in action creating harmony and peace. My Silent Master is Purity, so everywhere I stand, I can let my light dispel darkness. My Silent Master is Patience, so everywhere I interact, I can express my willingness to wait for my Love to harmonize and heal. I love who I am, and who I am reflects back to me in every person, every place, every action I perceive. Love and the ideas of Love are real and eternal. My Love can conquer all that is not real, just as light conquers darkness.

CHAPTER FOUR

LIFE EXAMINATION: DEFINING YOUR TRUE SELF

SILENT MASTER IMAGE II

YOU AND THE LIFE FORCE ARE ONE

Your Silent Master Consciousness was born out of the infinite Life Force creating and animating the Universe. You exist as a part of the Universe; therefore, It is the Life Force creating and animating you. It is the power that beats your heart. Because you are this Consciousness, whatever qualities the Life Force possesses, you possess also.

DISCOVER YOUR SELF TO DISCOVER LOVE

As I mentioned in Chapter One, the purpose of self-discovery is to discover freedom, to live free! In Chapters Two and Three we discussed some of the things you need to do to get ready for self-discovery and to commit your energy to the process. Now we look at the importance of closely examining the elements of your present life in order to create a new and better one, one designed to bring you greater freedom and happiness. This is the third stage of self-discovery: *life examination*. It is an essential part of the self-discovery process, and like *readiness* and *energizing*, it is a part of a process that really needs to be done every day, not just one time.

And why are we doing it at all? Because we want freedom! We want to be the original person we were born to be. And this means we must look at all the ways we may have strayed from our original self. How else can we get back on track?

As we begin to discover our original self and our original freedom, we will discover the heart of freedom: Love.

When you discover your true self and the freedom of your true self, you are discovering Love. Life without all the feelings and forms of Love isn't true life at all. Life without Love, no matter how full of material objects, is empty.

Perhaps you've noticed that many persons familiar to us in the media, famous musicians and actors, for example, often have enormous material success, yet sometimes end up in tragic circumstances, defeated by unhappiness, despair, loneliness, or suicide. Many times we think they have everything. But clearly they don't. Their lives tell us that where there is no love, there is emptiness, loss of freedom, and loss of life.

One of my favorite writings about Love is from the Bible:

> *If I speak in the tongues of men and of angels, but have not love, I am only a resounding gong or a clanging cymbal. If I have the gift of prophecy and can fathom all mysteries and all knowledge, and if*

*I have a faith that can move mountains, but have not love, I am
nothing. If I give all I possess to the poor and surrender my body to
the flames, but have not love, I gain nothing. Love is patient, love
is kind. It does not envy, it does not boast, it is not proud. It is not
rude, it is not self-seeking, it is not easily angered, it keeps no record
of wrongs. Love does not delight in evil but rejoices with the truth.
It always protects, always trusts, always hopes, always perseveres.
Love never fails . . . now these three remain: faith, hope, and love.
But the greatest of these is love.*

I CORINTHIANS 13:1–13

Whatever your material goals are, whatever goals you
eventually accomplish, if there is no Love there is no enjoyment, there is no pleasure, there is no fulfillment. That's
because the material fulfillment of a goal is impermanent.
The words of an angel, the sound of a gong or clanging cym-
bal — no matter how beautiful, loud, or impressive — do not
last. The sound comes and goes quickly. Just so, all things
material pass and are ultimately unreal, as we discussed in
the previous chapter.

But Love is eternal. Love is real. Love is really the only
goal, because it is the only fulfillment, the only happiness.
So, the real purpose of any goal you have in life is to find
Love. When you fulfill your goal, you will undoubtedly feel
the joy and Love within you.

You may think that love and joy come from achieving
your goal. The truth is that winning the goal awakened the
Love already within you. The real purpose for setting goals
and realizing them is to find the Love already within you,
which shines and survives through every material circum-
stance. After you find that Love and feel that joy, it's up to you
to keep it. Once you know it is within you, it is yours forever.

Have you ever noticed how a beautiful rainbow exists in
the air, as if it's really there? But if you try to go to it or touch

it, it moves away from you. That's how it is when we pursue material things ignorantly. Just when you grasp something or get something, you then want something else, and still something else. As long as you believe happiness is outside you, it will keep moving away from you. This kind of pursuit never brings satisfaction. But when you pursue material goals knowing that you're really discovering that Love within you, you can keep the Love that you find within you forever. Your material accomplishments are not unworthy, but they exist for the purpose of showing you the Love you already possess. By giving this love, and sharing it, you bring good to others as well as to yourself.

In this stage of self-discovery — *life examination* — we will look at your priorities. Are your current priorities leading you to Love that fills your life with peace and satisfaction? Or are you giving priority to things that keep you limited and unhappy?

You now have to take a hard and penetrating look at *who* you are and *where* you are. You then will be better able to define where you want to go. How close or how far are you from realizing the kind of life you desire to have? What have you gained over the years? What have you lost? What's in the way of being happy? What do you think you need? What do you need to eliminate? Are you moving in the best possible direction?

Death Is Right Beside Us

You may think those are fairly easy questions. After all, don't you look in the mirror every day and more or less size yourself up, plan your agenda? But these questions aren't as easy as you think, and most of us carefully dance around the honest answers to avoid confronting ourselves.

Many of us are seduced into a sense of "foreverness" about our lives, thinking that we have unlimited time to get somewhere or do something. Not that we say that consciously to ourselves. We don't say "I'm going to be alive forever;" we just act that way. We simply do not have the feeling from day to day that eventually we are going to die, or that our time here is limited.

Since we don't live from moment to moment with the awareness that we could die at anytime, we take our time answering the questions mentioned above, or we avoid them altogether. Even if we ask a question like "Am I where I want to be?" it's all too easy to reply "Well, I'll get there someday," and drop the matter right there. We tend to put off the fulfillment of our real goals to "when I retire," or "when the kids are out of the house," or "when I have time."

"Someday" is never going to come. The only time there is, is now. When "someday" comes, it will be *now.* So what you think and do right now is what will happen on the mythical "someday."

Unfortunately, death seems so mysterious, baffling, horrible, and final that we don't want to consider it in our daily lives. But we must have the courage to look squarely at the limited time frame death gives us, and act accordingly. You don't know when death will come. The "someday" you wait for may never come, simply because you won't be here to experience it!

Of course, as we discussed in the previous chapter, in reality what is really *you* will never die. Your Silent Master consciousness is eternal; only your manifestations — including your present body and life — come and go from your consciousness. So we're talking now about the death of your physical manifestation, and not of your eternal true self.

Death Is Part of Birth

The mystery surrounding the time of our exit from this life helps us concentrate on living instead of dying; but nevertheless, we must remain aware that since we have a limited time span, we need to reach for our goals now. We must always live now to the fullest because that is the only time we have.

Every *now* moment you experience is a birth, a new opportunity to think a new thought or take a new attitude. When you arrive on the earth, it is a birth, a chance to create a life. But each new day is also a birth. Each time you leave behind an old outmoded self-concept, it is a birth. Each time you create a new situation in your life, it is a birth. Birth and "death" are simultaneous events because something old has to "die" to give way to the new. This process goes on minute by minute, day by day, from the time you arrive until the time you leave.

In one sense death is necessary to create change. Learn to love change and to welcome it. One of the results of fear is a reluctance to accept change. Fear is an immobilizing feeling and tends to keep us where we are, no matter where that is. Perhaps we fear change because it indeed reminds us of death, and we don't welcome the death of anything, even the death of the old. But always remember that death is really birth because it is a change from the old to the new. See change as newness ever dawning, leading you from one opportunity to another.

ARE YOU WHERE YOU WANT TO BE?

If you are not where you want to be, now is the time to figure out where you want to go and how you're going to get there. But there is no point making plans until you know what you want. And to know what you want, you have to examine your priorities.

One of the exercises I give participants at my Self-Discovery Weekends is to ask: "*If you had only five days to live, what would you do in those five days?"* The way you answer tells you much about what your real values and priorities are.

Ask yourself that question now. Don't be surprised if you don't spend your last five days at your job or painting the house (which perhaps you may have done faithfully every weekend recently). Chances are you'll choose to do what really matters to you, what you really love, what is really you. Chances are you'll choose to be with your family or certain friends in a special way. Or perhaps you might choose solitude, experiencing nature's beauty in a private way. Or dancing. Or playing music. Answer for yourself, and then ask, "With every day that I do have now, how much time do I give to these things?" (After all, you could be living your last five days right now!)

The way that you answer that question gives you very important clues regarding your true direction in life. Your Silent Master consciousness speaks to you powerfully through your true desires. Of course I'm not talking about destructive or distorted desires like obsessive smoking and drinking. The desires you feel through the exercise above are most likely your true desires, and you have them for a reason. They tell you much about who you are as a unique individual and your unique role to play here on earth. Your desires will never be exactly like anybody else's.

Have you created a life that allows you to experience your own truths? Or have you created a life that has taken you so far from your inner truth that only during your last five days on earth will you allow yourself to experience what you love? If you find you are living here without enjoyment, without realizing your personal truth, then you have a right to change! That is what self-discovery is all about: fulfilling your true desires, not just thinking about them. As you find your true self, automatically you find your true place, your true activities, and your true fulfillment.

Re-identify Yourself

Whatever your life is right now, it is a result of how you have defined yourself, or how you have identified yourself. The personality you have, the way you identify yourself, is due primarily to two things: (1) the way you have allowed yourself to imitate someone else or have become a copy of others' expectations (instead of being your original self); and (2) the way you have expressed the need to acquire.

Others' Expectations

Let's talk about the first point — how you may have let go of your real self.

There is only one of you here. You are one of a kind — an original. How important it is, then, to be your original self, not a copy of someone else or a fulfillment of someone else's expectations.

The choices you have made about your personality traits and your career stemmed largely from the self-concepts you developed in your family, or wherever you grew up. We did not grow up alone. There were always significant people around us in the early stages of our lives teaching us who we are. How did they do that? By being our mirror. They told us things like, "I like you when. . . ." "You're bad when you. . . ." "You're too loud." "You're just like your sister." "Boys don't do that." "Good girls always. . . ." When you are a small child, your inner voice is powerfully overshadowed by the voices of the authority figures who literally determine whether you live or die. You quickly conform to their perception of you. If you reject their perceptions, then you are labeled "rebellious," which can be just as bad as accepting their other erroneous perceptions of you.

In short, very few of us emerge unharmed from the process of growing up. Even with the best intentions, parents —

or other significant caregivers — simply don't know your inner truth the way you do. No one can know your personal truth the way you do. Yet, everything in the environment of your formative years encourages you to silence your inner voice in order to please the persons you're dependent on.

If you were told — taught — that you are lazy, stupid, poor in math, beautiful, temperamental, athletic, friendly, shy, then you probably still are. Your caregivers didn't tell you that their opinions may have been faulty. Quite the contrary, to maintain their status as authority figures, they taught you that their word was law, and that only bad or rebellious children contradict them.

I invite you to a challenge. I am so confident that your true abilities far outweigh the self-concepts you have been taught that I am inviting you to try a simple experiment. Take one of the concepts you accepted from others as being "you." I realize this, in itself, is a challenge, because some of your learned self-concepts may be so ingrained that it wouldn't occur to you that you "accepted" them — you think of them as being "just the way you are." So try to be very honest as you do this.

Let's say you pick the characteristic of shyness. Go over your life — from two minutes ago to as far back as you can remember — and dig up those instances in which you were clearly not shy, those times you contradicted your belief entirely, and someone had an entirely different impression of you. I assure you that you will find at least one instance of this experience — probably more than one. Somewhere, some time, you'll find you acted totally differently from this belief, and someone was left thinking you were not at all shy. When you remember the incident — or incidents — you will recall a certain sense of calm and rightness that you felt. That calmness was you being you. Even if the incident was an angry moment when you left your shyness behind — still, there was a rightness to that moment when you acted from a true principle within yourself.

My point is that, no matter what trait you pick, there are instances when you did not demonstrate it. You may have already given up some of the "negative" traits that you were told you had, but you may still carry around the vague feeling of being "bad."

Therefore, don't let your personality, as it is now, define you. Realize you have been formed by others' opinions and expectations as much as or more so than your own inner knowing. Listen to your own inner voice and follow your own direction. The only truth is already in you, talking to you, being you. Let it come forth.

The Need to Acquire

The second reason why you may have lost yourself is the way you have expressed your need to acquire. Most of us are driven to acquire. We want material possessions.

There is nothing wrong with acquisition. Certainly we need to acquire a source of income to purchase necessities like clothing, food, and housing — what you might call the fundamentals of earthly life. So quite naturally, you formed a personality that could handle this need.

This personality is who you think you need to be in order to earn your way. Unfortunately, the formation of this personality did not necessarily and easily proceed from your inner truth. In most cases its formation proceeded from other people's opinions of you, their pressures and expectations, and many other social and psychological forces quite unrelated to your inner truth. But you quickly learned you had to acquire in order to live. You had to do what you had to do, you thought.

But life is not what you *have* to do. Life, as I'm teaching you now, is what you create. If you haven't created what you truly are, what you truly want, then now, right here in this now moment, is your chance to do so. *This means you will re-identify yourself. Instead of continuing along the path of your wrong identification with a limited and unreal personality, you will identify yourself as the manifestation of your unlimited and real Silent Master consciousness.*

You will continue to acquire, but only what you truly desire from within the knowing of your Silent Master consciousness. I like the biblical saying in Proverbs: "Wisdom is supreme; therefore get wisdom. Though it cost all you have, get understanding." When you find your true self, you can acquire anything that is good and right because it is already within you. Without the guidance of your true self, you will not acquire your highest and truest good. Searching for your true self is the way to create your optimum life path, because your true self is the seed of all you can become.

Here is a simple image to help you see what I mean. Imagine an acorn as the symbol of your life. In its simple form of being just a nut, it has value (just as you, in your roles right now, have value). But the value a simple nut has is not necessarily self-fulfilling. A nut has value as a food source for something else. It can be consumed. When that happens, its energy — its Life Force — is given over to something else, converted into energy that feeds another.

But imagine now that the nut refuses to be used by something else. Imagine that it chooses instead to fulfill itself, to pursue the path of self-discovery. Instead of being food, it gives itself food. It gives itself soil, and water, and sun, and time. What happens? That limited confining shell cracks and a tree grows. It develops into a growing, thriving life form with far more potential than it had as a simple nut.

I am encouraging you to do the same: Give yourself nourishment so that you may grow into a life form express-ing far more of your potential. If you are not where you want to be, stop identifying yourself with the limited personality you have, and re-identify yourself with your unlimited Silent Master consciousness.

Since you have spent a lot of time acquiring many elements in your life, part of the life-examination process is to examine what to keep and what to eliminate. Many material objects in your life are symbols of an undesirable past, or reminders of a situation you're trying to overcome.

One thing you can do to start overcoming the past is to eliminate the objects of the past from your environment. For instance, if you desire a life without drugs, is it wise to keep the objects involved in drug use in your home? If you are overcoming a problem with alcohol, should you keep liquor in your home? Are you keeping certain photographs, clothes, and pieces of furniture that are constant reminders of an undesirable relationship you're trying to dissolve? Keeping objects of the past in your present environment encourages you to continue identifying with the "you" of the past. This stands in the way of redefining yourself for a new life.

Identify with Your Silent Master Consciousness

The Silent Master Image at the start of this chapter says, "Your Silent Master Consciousness was born out of the infinite Life Force. . . . Because you are this Consciousness, whatever qualities the Life Force possesses, you possess also."

You and the Life Force are one. In order to express your power, you must identify with it. The purity, power, creativity, goodness, and wholeness of your Silent Master is within you now. So let's look at ways to strengthen your awareness of this connection.

As you go about re-identifying yourself, you will need a lot of patience and compassion. You have spent many years forging the personality you have, and you will now ask certain aspects of yourself to go.

Remember the old saying, "Don't go away mad, just go away"? That's the way you can regard old self-concepts as you replace them with more unlimited ways of thinking about yourself. You don't want to spend your energy criticizing and arguing with yourself. Instead, you can act from a clear, calm center within you to quietly take charge of directing your life.

Think about the compassion you feel for a little wounded bird separated from his mother and the shelter of his nest. Give yourself the same compassion as you go about healing yourself. You, too, have been separated from the shelter of your true self, and you deserve the same love and care to return you to safety.

Let's talk about your re-identification in five areas:

1. *Develop a stance of being the Silent Master consciousness, not becoming it.*

There is an important distinction between being and becoming. Remember, I said only the present moment, and not the future, exists in reality; therefore, the present moment is the only creative place for you to act. If you take a stance of *becoming*, you are placing your growth in the future, which is a time that never comes. If you take the stance of *being*, you place the truth of your being as here, right now in the present. You are now all that you ever can be.

All your strength, purity, will, potential, and ability is available now for your discovery and use.

As you stay in the now moment, refusing to allow emotions based on the future or the past to color your consciousness, you'll sense and know in every moment what is good, real, and right. These perceptions will cause you to take right action, and to be in the right place at the right time to bring about your optimum good.

You do not have to know intellectually what to do every moment, because the truth of your being already *is*. Since your Silent Master consciousness knows the best course for you to take, when you act you're not creating something out of nothing. Creating means to allow what already is in your consciousness to be. My job is not to tell you which ideas to bring forth. It is to tell you that your truth already is within you, and that you are responsible for bringing it forth.

You do this by listening in the present moment only to your own inclinations. Your Silent Master consciousness is constantly talking to you by giving you thoughts and inclinations that are accompanied by a feeling of rightness. We can call this "intuition." Intuition is not a mysterious, esoteric thing, but a normal, natural way of hearing the right direction voiced by your Silent Master consciousness. Again, however, you cannot hear properly if your consciousness is colored by emotions and thoughts surrounding the nonexistent past and future.

So, whatever you wish to "become," know that you have the potential to make it happen right now. By holding the concept firmly in mind through concentration and visualization (as we discussed previously), you help to bring it about.

2. Be willing to turn negatives into positives.

Many of us come from backgrounds in which there was trauma or abuse. For example, one woman talked to me about having been raped five years previously. The incident was still causing her much fear and depression, and she couldn't get over it. This was a big obstacle in her life because it was keeping her from knowing and experiencing any happiness. I told her that the rapist had probably long ago forgotten about the incident, but she was continuing to be raped over and over for five long years! Is that fair? Yet only she could do something about this injustice by disciplining her own mind.

Others talk to me about growing up in foster homes or living with an abusive alcoholic parent. But in all these examples, the negative situations or the traumas are over and gone! I am sorry that they happened, and so are they. And so is anyone who knows it was wrong. But now is the time to use those situations as fertilizer to create new situations and new growth. Even though you didn't have the power and control to stop the situation at the time it was happening, you have the power and control now to do something about it, to build something constructive on top of that event.

You may wonder how anyone could possibly find something constructive about being raped. How could anyone who was a victim of child abuse create something positive out of that? If you have trauma in your past, only you will know exactly how you can grow in a positive direction as a result. But speaking in general terms, here is something everyone can use to heal past trauma: You can learn to *let go.* People who learn how to release any and all negativity are flying with great speed toward freedom. There is little that makes you more free than knowing you don't have to feel the pain of negative states of mind, like hurt, anger, resentment, or jealousy.

The woman who was raped may not have had another incident in her life that could so forcefully teach her the power of releasing negativity, or the freedom of forgiveness. This does not mean she excuses the rapist's action, or justifies it, or believes it to be right under any circumstances. Instead, what it means is that she gains freedom and power when she doesn't allow harm to stay with her. You are very free when you know you are the guardian of your mind and act accordingly in all situations.

Here's a story I like to tell that illustrates the power of letting go and of turning negatives into positives.

There was once a fisherman who was always angry and miserable. He had no belief in the goodness of life, never expected any pleasure, never looked for any happiness. He never expressed any love or affection, and often vented his rage by beating his wife and children. His family was terrified of him, and everyone who knew him avoided him because of his wrathful behavior. His wife and children often wished he would never come back from his fishing trips.

One day, the fisherman left for the docks after his usual morning of screaming at his "lazy, good-for-nothing" children and railing at his wife for the breakfast that was never cooked right. Then, out at sea, the fish weren't biting, and the fisherman worked himself into an even meaner state. He cursed that he didn't deserve such a hard life and worthless family and how nothing ever worked out right for him.

He was so busy complaining he didn't notice that a dark storm had been building and was just about to turn violent. In a matter of minutes, massive ocean waves were writhing and churning furiously. His little boat was cast about like a helpless twig, and then suddenly the boat exploded into tiny pieces. The fisherman was cast into the water. Desperately he groped for the largest piece of the fragmented boat he could see, and he clung to it, struggling to stay afloat.

Meanwhile, the storm tore through the village as well. The fisherman's family was at home when it hit. Without warning, the roof suddenly crashed down upon them and flames shot out from the stove. Flames began engulfing the house quickly, and although they tried to put out the fire, all was to no avail. Frightened for her children's lives, the wife was almost more afraid of her husband's rage when he would return to find the house burned down. Still, she sent the children to the docks to look for him since he hadn't returned on time.

The children were likewise frightened as they ran to the docks. Even though they normally thought only of how they feared their father, now they truly worried that he was in danger. At the docks, they saw that most of the fishermen had returned safely, but their father was nowhere to be found. They called and waited.

At sea, the storm had finally abated. But it was totally dark. There in the black of night, the fisherman floated, weeping and clinging to the piece of wood, very, very alone. All his life he had been an angry man, taking for granted all that he had and complaining about everything. Now he was going to die alone in the middle of the darkness and a vast, compassionless ocean. Strangely, his thoughts turned to his family. He thought intensely about how he had never told them he loved them, and how he'd never taken any time with them. He really did care for them, and now he deeply regretted his miserable life and how he had never known any joy or warmth. At that moment, he wanted to be with his family more than anything in the world.

But where was the coast? He couldn't see in the darkness, so he couldn't tell which direction to swim. Tired and cold, he was ready to give up hope, but suddenly off in the distance he saw a faint glimmer. Yes, it was there, a small light off to the side. He started swimming toward the light. With each stroke, he began to plan how he was going to change things, how he was going to be the husband and father he'd never been. For hours the light guided him, until finally he began to see his fishing village in the distance. The light was bringing him home, so he pushed himself even harder.

Just as he was reaching the shore, he suddenly had a fear that maybe his family had been hurt or lost. But then he heard voices calling and saw his children rushing into the ocean toward him. They all wept as they embraced, and together they walked toward the house.

As the wife saw her husband approaching with the children, she was relieved, but she began to cry as she thought of how he would beat her when he saw the burned house. She saw his smiling face coming toward her, but she cowered, dreading the encounter. When he came near she timidly backed away, but to her surprise he reached out and embraced her warmly. She stammered as she tried to find words to tell him what had happened, but he wouldn't listen. As he held her tightly, he wanted only to tell her that the burning house had saved his life. "The flames shown through the darkness where I was lost at sea," he said lovingly, "and they guided me home! Now I have the chance I prayed for to be the husband you want and the father my children need."

Here we see how the fisherman, through a traumatic event, completely let go of the past in order to discover his true self again. He had "lost" himself long ago emotionally and mentally. And now he was experiencing the picture of that state of mind: he was "lost" at sea, floating around in the blackness. But the storm was a blessing in disguise. It was the thing that brought him back to life! Not sunshine, but rather a storm did it. Was it a trauma? Yes. But instead of giving up and drowning, he made the storm an opportunity to remember his true self. As a result, the only thing that drowned in the dark ocean was his misery and anger.

The family likewise experienced pain and despair. The burning house could have resulted in simply a destroyed home. Instead, the house was burning for a reason! The flames were the light of life to the fisherman. They brought him home again. So, in spite of the negative appearance of this seeming disaster, in reality everything worked together for good to bring love and healing. The negative situation turned into a positive one.

Here's something important to remember: This story ended in love and reunion instead of tragedy because the fisherman took action. Negatives don't automatically turn into positives. The house could have burned down for nothing. The fisherman could have died for nothing. If he had continued with his anger and defeatism and despair, he wouldn't have looked around to see the tiny flicker of light, and would surely have drowned. (When we look only at the dirt on the ground, we don't see the stars in the sky!) But instead, the fisherman changed his attitude, became open and receptive to a new state of mind. He felt remorse for the first time. And this action led to his perception of the light that saved his life.

Likewise, Love is behind all the events, even the obstacles in your life, and you can hold the right ideas as the fisherman did so that everything works together ultimately for good. Cling to the truth no matter what you see happening, and the truth you hold will transform your experience.

3. Develop detachment.

Detachment is the means by which you let go of the old in order to make room for the new. It is the means by which your good expands into greater good. As you redefine yourself, you will have to let go of old thoughts, emotions, and situations.

How do you let go? Whether it's a relationship, a job, an environment, a marriage, how is it possible to just let go? You may have already discovered it isn't an easy thing to do.

Detachment becomes easier if you remind yourself of one simple thing: everything material you create or draw to you with your thought and emotion is impermanent. All things material ultimately pass away, as we discussed in the previous chapter. Continuous change is the law of the universe. Detachment is the healthy way to regard everything you create, because it is simply an attitude in which you expect change. You look upon all you manifest as a creation, just that and nothing more. That way, whether you experience loss or gain, it doesn't matter, because you go on to create another situation and yet another.

Clinging to a good picture you have created possibly keeps you from expanding into an even greater good. Clinging to a disagreeable picture keeps you there! So, don't hold onto either as though it's the final story. You don't hate, resent, fight, or quarrel with an undesirable situation, and you don't overly love or cling to a desirable situation. Detachment means you are always ready, open, and willing to experience change. That is how you develop. You can't develop and grow if you hold on tightly to something you've acquired no matter how good you think it is.

If you are striving to redefine yourself by identifying with the peaceful consciousness of your Silent Master, you will need to detach from your turbulent emotions. Notice I didn't say not to have turbulent emotions. I said to detach from them. The way to eliminate turbulence from your consciousness is not to pretend it doesn't exist. Instead, you detach from it. When you feel it, you don't get into the feeling and run with it like a rider on a wild horse.

You see the feeling come into your consciousness, but you don't act on it. You consciously know that the emotion will pass through, leaving you unharmed if you refuse to interact with it. And you hold this idea so strongly that its energy actually cancels the emotion. Eventually, as you are in touch with more of your Silent Master consciousness, your energy will "burn up" those emotions as they enter your field so that you don't feel them at all.

For instance, let's say you feel angry when you find out someone has cheated you. If cheating has occurred, your idea of honesty can prevail to make this wrong situation right in some way. Your job is to take calm, appropriate action to correct the situation. Any anger you would be tempted to feel is of no value and no use. So you let it pass through you without acting on it. The only actions you take are those you are inspired to take as a result of focusing your energy on honesty rather than on dishonesty.

Detachment is inner freedom. It gives you the mobility you need to keep your thoughts free and clear; as a result, you free yourself from emotions that could cause you to take inappropriate action.

4. *Focus on creative attitudes like harmony, gratitude, and praise to bring love and beauty into the creation of a new you and a new world.*

I have mentioned how attitudes are like arrows that fly you toward your target goal — or away from your goal — depending on which attitudes you maintain. Positive attitudes are creative tools. Negative attitudes are destroyers. There's a parable in the Bible that beautifully illustrates this:

> *A farmer went out to sow his seed. As he was scattering the seed, some fell along the path, and the birds came and ate it up. Some fell on rocky places that did not have much soil. It sprang up quickly, because the soil was shallow. But when the sun came up, the plants were scorched, and they withered because they had no roots. Other seed fell among thorns, which grew up and choked the plants. Still other seed fell on good soil, where it produced a crop — a hundred, sixty, or thirty times what was sown. . . .*
>
> MATTHEW 13:3–8

The seeds in this story stand for your goals and aspirations. Seeds falling by the wayside and eaten by birds can be compared to an attitude of not valuing your goals, or allowing other interests or situations to distract you and "eat up" your energy and commitment.

Are your goals simply empty wishes, fleeting desires that quickly come and quickly go? Have you failed to take your goals seriously enough to make a plan or implement a strategy to fulfill them? If so, your goals are like the seeds that fell randomly by the wayside where the birds of distraction, neglect, and carelessness devoured them. Achieving goals requires a high quality of energy and commitment. You must make a plan and implement a strategy!

The seeds falling among stones and sprouting shallow roots are similar to allowing only shallow emotions to motivate or feed your goals. We usually begin working toward our goals with positive attitudes and the best of intentions. But if we haven't examined our goals and are being driven only by negative attitudes such as pride, guilt, depression, anger, or jealousy, then our soil is shallow. When the hot sun of adversity rises to challenge you with difficulties, that kind of energy will dry up and won't sustain you. Losing steam, you will find yourself turned away from your goal.

The seeds falling among thorns are like your goals being choked and killed by poor environments or by negative thoughts, feelings, and attitudes. When you are working toward new goals, you must be aware that your customary environment and the persons close to you may not be supportive of the changes you're making. Some acquaintances may fear your changes will harm their relationship with you, and they may, consciously or unconsciously, try to hold you back. You may find that your environment contains elements that work against your achievement. If you need to go to school to learn a new skill, will you have a quiet place conducive to studying? When you undertake a new challenge, give yourself the best environment you can, one that will be the least inclined to choke your efforts.

By contrast, when seeds fall on good ground, when your goals and aspirations are fed by positive attitudes, by your focus, your will, your energy, and your commitment, they are bound to grow and flourish. We all have the ability to be fruitful farmers in our lives. If we plant the seeds of our goals in the deepest and healthiest of soils, if we remove the weeds and stones that hamper our growth, if we nourish the growth with care and attention, then we are sure to see the blossoms and reap the fruits we desire.

Harmony, gratitude, and praise are particularly important attitudes to have. Why? Because all three attitudes acknowledge the presence of something. Why is this creative?

In order to manifest something, you must acknowledge that it exists as an idea. Harmony, gratitude, and praise have great creative power not only because you feel them only about something that exists, but also because they bring additional qualities to the manifestation.

For example, when you express harmony in your consciousness, you are acknowledging the presence of unity and peaceful interactions, and you bring these qualities into your manifestations. When you express gratitude, you are acknowledging the presence of value. So when you're grateful, you create something of value for yourself. With the attitude of praise in your consciousness, you are acknowledging the presence of beauty. You don't praise something that's ugly, do you? So praise brings beauty into your manifestations.

Even if these qualities did not have creative value, they would have value in improving the quality of life. Gratitude helps bring the beauty and pleasure of life sharply into focus. This story illustrates the power of gratitude.

Once there was a king who had grown very bored and disenchanted with life. He went from one meaningless and stagnant day to another, finding no satisfaction or pleasure in anything. He had even lost his taste for food, and all his traditional exotic dishes no longer yielded the joys they once had. He grew so tired and apathetic that he issued a proclamation that whoever could bring him a dish that truly pleased him would be richly rewarded.

The greatest cooks came from all over the world bringing their best dishes to be tasted by the king. But the king found none of them pleasing. Life continued to be one boring dish after another.

One day a poor farmer came to the palace to seek an audience with the king. When the farmer was finally called to appear, he said, "Your Majesty, I have the most incredible dish you've ever tasted. On this earth there is no other that can match it, but this special dish takes some very special preparation, and in order for you to fully enjoy it, I must ask that you eat nothing else until it is ready." The king didn't know what to make of this offer, but he was so bored with his food that he was willing to take a chance. He replied, "All right, farmer, I accept your offer, but your dish had better please me for all this inconvenience." So the farmer left to prepare his dish, saying, "It will, Your Majesty, it most surely will."

The next day the farmer arrived empty-handed in the king's hall. The king quickly asked, "Well, farmer, where is my food?"

"I'm sorry, Your Majesty. It will be ready soon, I promise, but you must still keep our bargain."

The next day the farmer again returned empty-handed. This time the king was furious. "Where is my food?" he roared. The farmer replied, his head bowed low, "Oh, Your Majesty, I'm still preparing."

"Still preparing?!" the king retorted. "I'm starving and you're still preparing?"

"I assure you this is the most fabulous food you've ever tasted," the farmer pleaded. "If you'll only wait one more day, it will be ready."

Although the king was angry and hungry, he was also anxious to relieve his boredom. "All right," he agreed. "One more day."

The next day the king awoke very early, his whole body filled with anticipation. He could think of nothing but the farmer's mysterious dish. When the time came near for the farmer to arrive, it was all he could do to contain his excitement.

Finally, from beyond his hall the king heard the light footsteps of the farmer. He smelled the most divine of smells. His whole body reverberated with incredible sensations of pleasure and delight. The farmer drew near. The king could feel his mouth salivating and his stomach grumbling as his entire attention focused on the farmer's simple porcelain bowl and its precious cargo.

The farmer lifted the lid to expose one thick slice of cabbage, steamed perfectly. It was the most simple of dishes, but at that moment, it was as precious as the world to the king.

The king bit into this pure, plain, and simple cabbage. Nothing in his life had ever tasted so good. His senses came alive as he felt once again the intense pleasure of taste, and smell, and texture. The king was so overjoyed that he made the poor farmer a rich man.

This king had dulled his senses through over-indulgence. Even though he had the best foods, eating had turned into something he did routinely day after day, something he just took for granted instead of experiencing the quality and care of what was prepared for him. As a result, he had no appreciation for that aspect of his life, no gratitude, no pleasure. Even the tangiest, spiciest food could not stimulate him; everything tasted flat, uninteresting, and unexciting.

Only when he was deprived of the object of his over-indulgence — his food — was he able to sharpen his senses again and remember the uniqueness of tasting and appreciating something simple. The cabbage by itself was not exciting. The cabbage alone could not restore the king's senses. Instead, it was his anticipation of the unknown "incredible" dish that excited him, and it was the feeling of appreciation from lack of food that stimulated him. Through fasting, the king corrected the stagnation caused by over-indulgence, and he was then able to feel gratitude and appreciation once more. Experiencing those feelings again, the king was overjoyed and was restored to his normal self.

Gratitude is not only a creative attitude, but also it brings joy, excitement, and energy into your life.

5. *Have a plan.*

Once you know what you want, make a specific plan of how you're going to get it. And make your plan visible. Write it out. Put it on a sign. Put it on a tape recorder. Know clearly what intermediate steps you're going to take to get there. This may seem like such an obvious thing to do, but you might be surprised how many people stop short of making such a plan. How many times have you said, "I'm going to . . ." or "I want to . . ." and never did anything about it?

Sometimes you stop short of making a plan because you honestly don't know what to do. This is where visualization can help you. Remember, your Silent Master consciousness is ready to energize your every thought and feeling into form. When you don't know what to do, take the visualization of your completed goal to your Silent Master in the type of meditation described in Chapter Three. Your Silent Master will see and hear the visualization, and in order to bring it forth, it will tell you what to do. You may get a feeling or an intuition of a specific action to take, or someone may suddenly come into your life to start the process, or you may feel an inclination to go somewhere or call someone. The point is, by continuing to hold the visualization and by listening receptively to your inner knowing, all the details will gradually manifest. Once you do know what to do, it's up to you to follow through with commitment and perseverance.

If you have established your priorities, identified your goals, and identified yourself with the power of your Silent Master, you are ready to make your aspirations come to life! In the next chapter, we look at the fourth stage of the self-discovery process: rebirth, where you start living the truth of your real self. Every challenge is an opportunity for rebirth into a new you. And victory is your birthright!

PRACTICE

ONE

Here is an exercise to help you see where you have placed your priorities in your relationships. Let's say you have five days left to live. You have set aside at least one of those days to say goodbye to certain people — to relationships — you presently have or have had in the past. First of all, who are the people you want to speak to at the end of your life? Children? Parents? Siblings? Spouse? Old friends? Co-workers? And what will you say to them? Write your message to each of them, freely, honestly. Then look closely at what you say. Do your words indicate you may have missed knowing them altogether? Do your words indicate regrets? Anger? Unexpressed gratitude? Unforgiven deeds? Words you've never said, but wish you had? Or is your goodbye filled with peace and love?

What do you discover about your attitudes in this exercise? What changes would you like to make?

TWO

What is a specific goal that you have? Make a mental "video tape" of you being there, doing what it is you desire. For instance, if your goal is to learn to fly an airplane, see your-self as already having your license. Clearly see yourself arriving at the airport, getting into your plane, taking off, and flying into whatever adventure you want to create.

The purpose of this exercise is to help you propel the goal into form, and to develop your power of visualization. Therefore, use all your senses. Hear the noise at the airport, the sound of the engine, the sound of the airplane door slamming. Talk to people, hear what they say to you. Smell the fuel and the air, and feel the wind blowing, the sun shin-ing, and the heat of the sun through the window. See the clouds in the sky, the color of your clothes, the patterns on the ground as you look down.

The clarity of visualization improves with practice. So enjoy the process of becoming more expert and getting more and more detail into your visualizations.

MEDITATION

Right now I am at one with the Consciousness that is the crea-tive force of all that exists. I am that Consciousness. My ideas turn into form in unlimited ways that express the goodness, purity, perfection, wholeness and unity of the Life Force of the entire universe. I am, therefore, a co-creator of all that exists. I am allowing the good and pure ideas of the Silent Master consciousness to flow through my consciousness smoothly, easily, and without obstruction, and to turn into beautiful and pure forms. I am open and receptive to my truth within. The truth within me helps guide me to take right actions everywhere I am every moment.

CHAPTER FIVE

REBIRTH:
LIVING YOUR TRUE SELF

SILENT MASTER IMAGE VI

YOU ARE COMPLETE, PEACEFUL, AND FULFILLED

Your Silent Master expresses completeness, fulfillment, harmony, peace, joy, and love, and imparts these qualities to everything It creates.

Now we have arrived at the fourth stage of self-discovery: *rebirth*. In the first stage, the readiness stage, we looked at how to get control of your thinking so you could begin to shape your thinking and your environment; in the second stage, the energizing stage, we looked at ways to purify your thinking and environment so that you could utilize more of your natural power and energy as you shape your life; in the third stage, the life-examination stage, we looked at how you can redefine yourself in order to bring out your true self, and to get on and stay on the path you desire. Now we look at the rebirth stage, in which you actually *realize* — make real — your goals and objectives. This stage is a culmination of the first three, and like the first three, it happens on a daily basis, even moment by moment.

SELF-DISCOVERY IS "SELF-UNCOVERY"

One of the most exciting things about self-discovery is the changes you see in your life as you continue to take charge of your thinking and environment. You may find yourself suddenly wondering, "Is this me wanting to change my career? Sell my house? Move to another state?" When you begin to feel your true self, you may experience many new ideas and may want to take actions that are completely out of the ordinary for you. A big change may feel like a rebirth into a new you.

When you begin to see yourself in your natural purity, you will notice one thing for sure: you are an original. There is no one exactly like you. You were born with all the unique qualities and capabilities you need to fulfill your own purpose and destiny. If people and conditions in your environment have made you become a copy of someone else's expectations, it doesn't matter. It's never too late to find your self. Your real self is still there waiting to be discovered. What is real and true about you can never be destroyed. Only what's false about you can be destroyed. What is really and truly you is here right now and will be with you forever.

Let's take a closer look at what discovery means. Discover means to *uncover*. When something is discovered, it is uncovered so that you can see what's really there. When Columbus discovered North America, he found something that was already there. He did not invent North America; he uncovered the ignorance about the shape of the globe and found North America, which nobody in Europe had imagined. It's the same when you seek your Silent Master. Self-discovery does not mean inventing new things about you or making up a new personality, but uncovering what you already are in your natural purity.

Rebirth Is Transformation

Since your true self is generally not uncovered all at once, self-discovery is a process of being born over and over again as more of your potential is outwardly expressed in your life. If you've ever watched a plant grow from a seedling to a flower, you've seen how its growth takes place in many stages — its size, color, and form change from day to day. The growth is so gradual that you probably don't consider the transformation as one birth after another. But it is. The plant is being reborn constantly in one little change after another, until it fulfills its potential and finally takes on a form completely different from the little sprout at the beginning.

In Asia, the cultivation of rice is often seen as a symbol for human life, as it goes through many transformations. First, there is the tiny tip that shoots up, like infants opening our eyes for the first time. Next the tips grow tall enough to wave in the breeze, delicate, but strongly reaching upward, like the way we hungrily and innocently explore our new world when we're young. Then the rice starts to develop its mature form, drinking in water and sun, which is the way we begin to grow as we assume our identities, and our minds open and develop. Finally, the rice ripens and stands up straight, full and rich. This is how we desire to be at the peak of our lives, self-confident and in control of body, mind, and spirit. Then at last, the rice stalk bends low due to the weight of its fruit. This is a symbol of humility, a respectful bow to the Life Force that has brought us here. We realize the universe is more vast and eternal than our simple physical life span here. And if we have really been at work on the lessons of life, we humbly realize how much we have to learn. There's never a place for arrogance; there is always so much more to discover.

Like the rice, you have moved through many stages to come to this point in your life. And you will have many more rebirths as you change your thinking and see new situations spring up in your life.

At this stage of the self-discovery process — rebirth — I emphasize the inner power step of *Love*. As we discussed in the previous chapter, Love is at the heart of freedom, the ultimate goal we're working for. I also emphasize the inner power steps of *Loyalty* and *Patience*, because as old self-concepts give way to the new, different obstacles will undoubtedly arise to challenge you. New distractions may appear to take you away from your goals, and you will need to remain loyal to yourself and to your commitment. And only with the right sense of patience will you be able to stick to your goals long enough to see them bear fruit.

First, let's look at how Love is involved in your many rebirths throughout life, and then we'll consider how Loyalty and Patience are so important in true self-discovery.

LOVE

Your Silent Master within is the same Life Force that created the universe. And this Life Force is pure Love. Everything it creates expresses Love. Although we may always remain humbled by the vastness of this infinite Life Force, we should always remember we are at one with it. The universal Life Force brought the universe and all of us into being with Love. And it is the power of Love that moves us from one rebirth to another in life as we transform by discovering more of our true Silent Master within.

Love Is the Universal Life Force, Your Silent Master

When you find real Love in your life, you have a special feeling of happiness that is not dependent on anyone or anything in order to be. That's because it comes *from* you, not *to* you from outside sources. This Love, which is within you now, is your Silent Master consciousness. When you express this Love, you are expressing your Silent Master.

It's a quiet joy, but also one that expresses great enthusiasm. When you feel this Love, you're glad to be alive, and grateful to wake up every day and live your life. This Love finds beauty everywhere, and appreciates how creative life is, knowing that possibilities exist everywhere to create more joy and more happiness and more freedom. This Love can't be hurt or destroyed because it is pure energy. It can be temporarily clouded over, but not destroyed. When it is clouded over with negative emotions or painful situations, it keeps on loving until harmony is reached again.

Because this Love is real and true, it is powerful. It can overcome anything untrue simply by being there, just as the sunlight burns clouds away. As an example, one of my students once had to visit a hostile enemy, someone who had

tried to take violent action against him. My student was naturally scared of the meeting, and talked to me about it. I told
him that no matter what this person says or does, don't get
angry, don't react. Just love him. Just feel love and know that
this person is acting out of ignorance and is not being his
true self. Just love, no matter what. My student went to the
meeting and, sure enough, the person yelled and screamed,
beat on the desk, beat on the wall, threatened, intimidated,
but my student remained calm and loving. Pretty soon, his
enemy just gave up. Where there is love, there is no opening
for anything else to get in.

I want to emphasize that this is perhaps easier said than
done. To really love in this way requires great discipline and
self-control. But every time you practice loving, you get better at it! Every time you see the result of the power of love,
you are encouraged to do it again. And then you find yourself rising to higher and stronger levels of being. Take advan-
tage of hostile or aggressive situations to prove the strength
of Love.

Love Accepts Challenges

At the rebirth stage, I emphasize the inner power step of Love
because rebirth, or just plain growth, is not always easy or
pleasant. When you understand how Love works, you know
everything you're doing is creating good, and not just making
life more difficult.

A difficult challenge or any kind of adversity can be a
good thing. Sometimes in my class I deliberately create
difficult or uncomfortable situations for students. Comfortable situations won't always bring out weaknesses, and I want
students to see their weaknesses so they can do something
about them. Eliminating weakness makes you stronger.

Sometimes new students will say, "I don't have any problems ... I don't feel insecure or weak ... I'm just here to get

some exercise. . . ." Then, after a little bit of training, I hear, "I didn't realize I was afraid of this . . ." or "I didn't know I had all this anger inside. . . ."

Love is a pretty thorough housecleaner and sometimes expresses itself through what seem to be unloving situations. After you make a conscious effort to transform and grow, Love will wash out some qualities you may not enjoy seeing up close. You may find your generosity is really a desire to win favor, or you may find your unselfishness is really weakness. You may find your patience is really laziness.

Like the stalk of rice bending over because of its fullness from the lessons of life, it will require some humility to be willing to see these things in yourself, and some strength and commitment to make a change. So you must love yourself enough to know that Love is always there for you, and stay true to yourself until Love — your Silent Master — shows you the good by clearing away the falsehoods. Be able to bend like the rice when you confront undesirable qualities in yourself. It's because the rice is flexible that it doesn't break when the wind blows.

Sometimes people find that their life really "heats up" only after they've made the decision to change or to grow for the better. Their life previously may have been quiet and uneventful, and at first glance, it may seem that the old life was better. But was the old life quiet and uneventful? Or was it stagnant? Let's take a lesson from nature. Which is the water you want to drink: the water from a running river, or water from a stagnant pond that's been sitting, unmoving, for years and years? Self-discovery and growth is like the running river — always moving somewhere. But running water is bound to meet obstacles, so it goes over and around them to follow its course. When you make the decision to discover your true self, your thoughts and emotions change, and your life moves like a running river. And Love will bring changes to you in all kinds of ways, not just in ways that previously seemed like fun.

Trust the Power of Love

What is trust? Isn't trust acknowledging the presence and reality of something? When you trust your Silent Master, you're trusting that its truth and love are real and present. If trust doesn't come easily, you may have to use some self-discipline to learn to trust, which we will discuss shortly.

If you have trouble trusting, you will tend to feel fearful and powerless when you have to deal with obstacles that seem beyond the power of your physical self to cure. But think: Could the Life Force that created the universe and created you be so unreliable as to leave you stranded in any situation? Isn't your Life Force beating your heart right now? Your Silent Master — the universal Life Force — is the closest thing to you. It is your breath, your heartbeat, and your warmth. All over the world, new life of all kinds is being born, showing us over again how life comes into being by itself.

Since the Life Force exists eternally, everywhere, with or without you, trust is something only you can do. You can choose to acknowledge the Life Force as your own, and act as one with it. Or you choose to ignore it, in which case you can't use it, and you will feel powerless.

Trusting your Silent Master is one of the ways you make your connection to the universal life force real and powerful and *present*.

Imagine a bird committed to flying toward an important destination in some rough, but manageable, weather. He is flying to a reunion with his long lost true love, so it's pretty important that he gets there. The bird may be thinking, as we do in similar situations, "Well, this weather isn't so bad. It's not the best, but I can handle it. . . ." Suddenly, the winds turn fierce and toss the bird all around. The wind now seems to be in control. The bird is pushed and pulled and thrown in every direction. He thinks, "I'm doomed. I can't win against this. I'll never get there. Why did this happen? Why me?" We have this typical reaction to obstacles in life all too often.

At this point the bird can believe his own words, accept the limitation, and drop to the ground.

But let's say this is a trusting, self-disciplined bird. He quickly catches himself in this limited thinking, and focuses instead only on the goal — his destination. He refuses to be distracted from his goal by mere obstacles and delays, and refuses to engage in blame, criticism, self-pity, anger, or any kind of vengeful, retaliatory thoughts. All he says is, "My wings are still working, so I will keep flying no matter what." Then, the fierce winds blow even harder, so hard that the bird is thrown up and up over the clouds, where he finds the calm, still air above the storm. Suddenly he can fly better than before, without obstruction. The wind that was his obstacle becomes the very thing that lifts him higher, to where he is free and unhindered in pursuing his goal.

This story shows what I mean by trusting in the power of Love. When you trust in it, Love will be there for you no matter what forms appear or disappear on the face of Love. Whatever storms and obstacles you encounter as you fly toward your goals, Love is available to you.

Whether the fierce wind was a bad force or a good force — an obstacle or a help — was up to the bird. He made the choice. Since he chose not to regard the wind as an undefeatable obstacle, Love, as it always will, empowered him to transform the situation. When the bird was lifted above the storm, he experienced the results of his own disciplined thinking, attitude, and expectations. If he had responded to his first set of thoughts, feelings, and expectations, he would have dropped to the ground and would never have met his true love at the end of the journey.

Just as storms appear in nature and temporarily cover the sun, emotional storms will appear in your life and temporarily cover your Love. How do you discover the Love behind your storms and obstacles? Through self-discipline.

Self-discipline is the way you respond to obstacles and challenges. Self-discipline means making good choices, so that you don't stray from your goals when the going gets tough.

Loyalty

Loyalty is the self-discipline that allows you to always remain committed to yourself and your goals. Loyalty to yourself means that you won't give in to self-defeating temptations. I emphasize the inner power step of loyalty during the rebirth phase of self-discovery because all kinds of distractions may tempt you away from your goals; only if you love yourself enough to remain totally disciplined and loyal to yourself can you win your victory.

Self-discipline is like a sharp sword that cuts away the attachments that keep you from being loyal to yourself. When you are disloyal, don't you respond to something that has a hold on you? You could never be disloyal — to yourself or anyone or anything — unless there was something attached to you that you let have power.

You must be able to clearly identify those things that tempt you or that have power over you. Olympic athletes in training become aware of what interferes with their workouts and avoid those distractions. A person indulging in destructive jealous behavior, for example, must identify and understand the reasons for the jealousy in order to correct the condition. So, awareness is a very important partner to self-discipline.

Self-discipline is the way you detach from the things that exercise power over you. *You* must be the center of power, not things in your relationships or your environment. As you develop self-discipline, you will need to develop the quality of detachment (see Chapter Four).

Detachment Means Letting Go

When we talk about the ability to let go, we can view it on two levels: physical and mental. Both are related, of course, because your physical life is a picture of your mental life. Detachment means letting go of both outer material things and inner attitudes. First, let's consider what detachment means in your outer, physical life.

Remember that your thoughts and emotions help create the environment you live in. When you allow new ideas — or new concepts or new expectations — to live in your mind and feelings, this tends to create new situations in your environment. Once you tune into your Silent Master, you will more often feel desires and inclinations that reflect your true purpose. Those desires and inclinations may be totally different from everything you've experienced before, and may take form as big changes in your life, because your goals necessarily change, your priorities change, and you take very different actions than before. Every time you conquer a fear or overcome a weakness you become a different person — a more true and powerful person.

What happens with every new birth you experience? Something old dies. That is the way it has to be. When you change, the old and the new cannot exist side by side. If transforming yourself sometimes has a price, this is it: You can't always keep what's familiar. When you start something new, it isn't always comfortable or easy to let go of the past. You may want to lose weight, for example, and maybe you've started to do so. But how do you respond when you realize that now the old eating habits have to go — permanently — in order to win your goal? Or maybe you want to enjoy a new circle of friends you have met at night school, but how easy is it to give up the old circle of friends who presently claim all your time?

This is where self-discipline comes in — when you are ready for a transformation. You will sometimes have to consciously and intelligently choose to let go of a person or situation in order to pursue your true goals. Are you familiar with the story of the monkey who has his hand on some food inside a hole? Suddenly, he sees something he wants more, outside the hole. But he can't grasp the new object because he doesn't realize he has to let go of the object inside the hole to get his hand out. He keeps pulling and tugging, trying to get his hand out, and doesn't realize he won't succeed until he lets go.

Self-discovery means you always have to question your priorities, readjust them, and then let go of what you don't want, even if it's comfortable and familiar. This will affect your relationships, and your environment as well. For example, if you find you're holding onto a house or some other piece of personal property that keeps you from taking an action you truly desire, you may have to intelligently and consciously let it go.

Detachment Means Controlling Your Mind

Letting go of attitudes is just as important as letting go of physical things. In fact, unless you let go of certain attitudes, your physical letting go won't last very long.

Sometimes it seems easier to use your will power to change physical habits than to change mental habits. You can control your body with your will power to make your body carry out your wishes, but your mind seems to act all by itself: thoughts and pictures seem to come and go without your invitation or consent. You have to learn to treat your thoughts and mental images as though they are subject to your control.

Whatever you hold in your mind in the present moment tends to be created in your life. Are you holding onto yesterday's grief, anger, and resentment, or feeling fear and depression about tomorrow? Only by strictly observing the content of your mind can you control the thoughts which, in turn, will take form as your reality.

Here's a story that illustrates how we choose the content of our minds, and how we must not let our thoughts rule over us.

A master and his student were traveling through the country to reach their temple. One of the vows in their sect was to never touch a member of the opposite sex. When they came to a stream, they found a young maid who was stranded, unable to cross the river. She was desperate to reach the other side. Feeling compassion, the master picked up the woman and carried her to the other side. He then traveled on with his student, but in silence, because his companion had turned sullen and withdrawn.

After walking several miles, the student was unable to hold back his anger. "How could you do that?" he blurted out, without disguising his disapproval and anxiety. "Haven't you always taught me never to touch a woman? And now, without a thought, you do the very thing you taught me is wrong. Surely you have sinned." The master remained calm and serene. "I left the woman on the bank of the river," he replied. "Why are you still carrying her?"

This story shows how the thoughts we keep in our minds can rule over us as long as we allow them to stay there. The master who was able to let go of the action he took to help the woman had a pure mind. He understood that the purpose of the vow not to touch a woman was to help keep his mind free of sexual desire. Since his intent was simply to show compassion, and not to feel sexual desire, he knew that he was not being impure and was not breaking the spirit of his vow. Naturally, under those special circumstances, it was easy to let go of the action he took once it was completed.

The student chose to mull over the situation, criticizing and resenting, and did not demonstrate the same purity of mind. He didn't look any deeper than the surface of the situation to see the purity of his master's action, and instead he looked only at the "sin." As a result, he couldn't let go of the scene in his mind.

If the master and student were presented with a real temptation to give in to a seductive woman, who do you think would be more likely to do it — the master, who seemed to go against his vow to touch a woman, or the student, who made such an issue out of the "sin"?

Perhaps you'll agree that the student would be more likely to give in to temptation. Why? Because he demonstrated that sin and temptation were more powerful in his mind than purity was. How did he demonstrate that? By keeping the sin active in his mind, where someday it could easily take form. He could have chosen instead to concentrate on purity, as his master did, but he let the sin be more vivid to him.

Attachments Can Be Obstructive

Since you know that your thoughts and emotions help create your environment, here's a warning: If your thought, emotion, or attitude binds you to a person or a situation, you make change impossible. What are the ties that bind? Anger, hate, resentment, criticism, jealousy, lust, hurt (self-pity), to name just a few. It's a common misconception that most of our attachments center on objects, and that we have to get rid of material objects to get rid of attachments. The truth is, our attitudes and feelings about the objects are more binding than the objects themselves.

For example, we may feel attached to an object, a person, or a situation because we like feeling comfortable and fear change. In this case fear is the attachment, not the object itself. If we fear the unknown, then we tend to cling to what we have, and remain afraid of anything new. Unfortunately, we will even cling to something that hurts us, whether it's an object or an attitude.

Let's take resentment. This is a common mental attachment most of us have to deal with at some time or other. And it really is an attachment. If you think about the last time you were resentful, you probably thought you had every right and every good reason to feel that way, and it didn't occur to you to give it up. Most likely you were completely unaware how your attachment to that resentment was quite destructive.

Let's say someone else got the promotion you thought you deserved. Maybe you became resentful, and found yourself thinking, It isn't fair. That person isn't as good as I am. I should have that job, not her. And maybe you even thought, I hope she fails, because she doesn't deserve it. Then you allowed those thoughts to dwell in your mind with lots of strong feeling attached, and you probably felt very justified because you felt you were so right.

The fact is, the feeling of resentment is totally unnecessary, and by feeling it, you put yourself in your own prison. You take away your ability to create your own good.

How so? Let's take a closer look at what you hold in your mind when you allow resentment to dwell there. When you say "It isn't fair," you're overlooking the fact that thoughts and emotions create everything that exists for you. Don't misunderstand when I say this: You don't get what you deserve in this instance; you get what you are. Whether or not you think you deserve something is not important. The feeling of deserving something is often a matter of human judgment, which can be faulty. What you *are* in your thinking is important because that's where the creative power is. When that person got the promotion you wanted, it means she helped create it or attract it. Just because she got that position doesn't mean you won't get one commensurate with your worth. But at that moment, she, not you, manifested the job. By resenting it, you're saying that you don't have the power to create your own situation. You're denying your own power, and you're giving it to the other person instead.

And that brings me to a second point. When you say "I should have that promotion, not her," you're saying that there are a limited number of promotions to go around. So what if that person got the position you wanted? Why limit yourself and stop there? You can get what's right for you, as well. Maybe it's not time yet. What if another, better job is taking form right now? It's possible the reason you didn't get that promotion is because it would prevent you from being available for a better job. But, by resenting, you're saying that only *one* person can get a good job.

When you say, "I hope she fails because she doesn't deserve it," you're saying that good can be destroyed or taken away from people. If you believe that, then you're making yourself a victim of the belief as well. The feeling of resentment hangs in your mind, covering your life like a gloomy umbrella.

By resenting this person, you're also hanging onto all the other negative beliefs that will keep you in state of loss. As long as you hold that resentment, as long as you have that attachment, you will not be free to use your thoughts and emotions to create your own good. These false beliefs will create more negative situations, which will encourage you to feel more resentment, and the cycle will go on and on until you stop it. How do you stop it? By understanding why you must let go of those mental qualities, and then by using your will and intelligence to do it.

Since holding resentment can prevent you from focusing your energy on your own good, doesn't it make sense to give it up?

For practice, think about a few other negative qualities like anger and self-pity or whatever you might be holding right now, and analyze the beliefs that go with those feelings, just as I did for resentment. I think you will easily convince yourself of the need to let go of negative attitudes if you want to create new good in your life.

An Open Mind Helps Remove Unwanted Attachments

One of the things we are most attached to is our point of view. This particular attachment makes it difficult for us to understand the feelings and motivations of others. Sometimes in my seminars I hold up an ordinary object like a cup or cassette and ask four people to sit around me and describe what they see. I encourage them to freely speak their minds. Before long, they're arguing with each other about what the object "really" looks like because their points of view are so radically different. From this exercise, they get an opportunity to experience how a person's point of view is typically quite inflexible, and how one will emphatically argue without really listening to anyone else.

An open mind means that we are willing to consider other points of view, and that we will take other perspectives into consideration before drawing iron-clad conclusions or making black-and-white judgments. This open-minded stance will not only help us get along better with each other, but will also help us intelligently evaluate the quality of our government, our leaders, and our laws.

Possess Without Being Possessed

How much stress is in your life because of the struggle to prevent loss or change of some kind? How much of your precious time is stolen from you because you constantly have to manage, care for, repair, or clean objects that are not that important?

If you can be surrounded by objects, persons, or events without fear of losing them, and if you really understand that all material things are impermanent and are subject to change, loss, and gain, you are on your way to true freedom.

Since everything material sooner or later will disintegrate, you will find your truest freedom in discovering happiness and satisfaction apart from possessions. Yes, we live in a material world where we need material objects for survival, but we do not need to be attached to those objects for happiness. Happiness is a quality you already possess within your Silent Master consciousness, which can never be shaped by material loss or gain. The more you strive to release yourself from attachment to material objects and limited thinking, and find this true state of happiness within, the more indestructible your freedom will be.

Patience

I emphasize the inner power of patience during the rebirth stage because you are bound to make mistakes as you try to bring out new aspects of yourself. You also need patience to help you wait for the outcome you desire to create. Patience involves love and loyalty. Waiting doesn't mean sitting back and hoping; waiting means loving yourself enough to patiently stay loyal to your truth until your outcome is manifested. Whether you're trying to find a new career, create a better relationship, or lose weight, patience will be necessary as you work toward your goal.

Patience is so important in the rebirth stage of self-discovery that I tell a story to illustrate the perils of impatience. Just as you used self-discipline to remain loyal to your goals, you need mental discipline to overcome the enemies of patience.

Once there was a village whose people had never seen an apple tree or eaten an apple. One day a stranger came to the village and presented them with their first apples. They tasted the fruit, and they were awed and inspired by the strange but wonderful and delicious taste. "How can we have this?" they asked with desire and enthusiasm. "What can we do to obtain fruit like this?" The stranger replied, "Believe it or not, you can grow this fruit from these tiny seeds."

The stranger showed them tiny seeds altogether different from the fruit they had just eaten, and invited the villagers to plant them. Seven excited would-be apple farmers came forward, took the seeds, and planted them. They all worked very hard to do everything the master told them to do for planting, because each of them really wanted a crop of luscious red apples. Each began dreaming of the day they would taste the apples.

Isn't that how you react when one day you finally realize what you want out of life, and you also realize you can get it? Just as the stranger showed them the means to get the desired apples, you have learned that there are specific tools (such as those in this book) to help you reach your goals. The process of self-discovery — or as in this story, the process of apple farming — then begins, and you're on your way with excitement and anticipation.

Days passed and nothing happened. One would-be farmer started to get discouraged. Already it had been over a week and no apples had appeared. Then one day a tiny green stem started to poke its head up through the soil. The farmer was furious. "This sprout doesn't remotely resemble an apple tree," he grumbled. Thinking of all the hard work he put into tending the field, he stomped on the plant, and marched off in a huff, discouraged, disillusioned, and angry.

Now we begin to see the problem of impatience. Instant results are wonderful, but the problem is, they seldom exist. This farmer's impatience was a result of not trusting the growing process. He didn't trust that an apple tree would come after the sprout if only he could wait patiently during the period of development. Instead, after waiting only a short time, he abandoned the project because he didn't have a completed apple.

Are you that kind of farmer? We seldom get instant results when we work on developing ourselves. You may see only a little change at first. But the little change should be a big reminder that change is happening, and that your full growth will surely come if you have patience. That's all that matters. The speed at which you grow does not matter. If you are trying to overcome your shyness with the opposite sex, for instance, be happy with yourself if you find you can look at someone with interest. Then you can be happier still when you are able to actually start a conversation. Be happy with small steps until you reach your goal.

Many weeks passed, and the trees belonging to the other farmers sprouted branches and started growing rapidly. But one farmer started to grow weary of the routine, getting up every day so early to water, remove the weeds — every day so much work. After a while he became preoccupied with other things he was doing, and started forgetting to come to water and weed. Finally, one day when he remembered to visit his tree, he found it had withered from lack of water and care. At first he was heartbroken, but soon he was preoccupied again with all the other things that had kept him busy.

Here we have another kind of impatience: the inability to remain committed long enough to see the goal come to fruition. Are you that kind of farmer? He started out with the best efforts, and ultimately even regretted his negligence, but he lacked the fiery energy to stay loyal to his goal and continue the work until the apples manifested. He drives home the lesson of remaining loyal to the objective, resisting distractions that take you away from your goal.

Remember that we discussed the best way to resist distractions — to let go of what distracts you. That farmer proved he was able to detach, but he detached from the wrong thing. He let go of his goal! And he had only himself to blame. Stay loyal to your goals.

Months passed and the small trees grew higher. Now they stood as tall as the farmers and were starting to fill out. The growth had seemed to take a long time, and one farmer was starting to feel a little aggravated. He had given up so many things for this tree, he thought. He was no longer able to do all the things he had done before. His friends would stop by and want to go places, but often he had to stay and take care of his tree. Many friends had been laughing at him, wondering why he was wasting away his life on the stupid tree. Now more and more he was asking himself the same thing: Why am I he doing this? Finally, he decided that the tree had become a prison to him. He kicked it down and went off to be with his friends, feeling free and yet somehow strangely empty inside.

I hope you won't fall prey to that farmer's type of impatience. He couldn't remain clear as to what his priorities were. His impatience — or giving up — was a result of not clearly defining what he wanted. You either want an apple tree or you don't. You either want self-discovery or you don't. If you do, then that goal has to remain a priority until the goal is won. You don't respond to temptations and distractions, no matter what their source.

When you make something a priority, you go beyond *trying* to win the goal. Merely trying puts your desire into the future, which you will always be in the process of trying to reach someday. Instead, a commitment to a priority means you see yourself already there. You keep that vision until you are there. The farmer lost his vision by giving power to distractions that gradually took hold of him. No wonder he felt strangely empty when he walked away from the tree. When you give up a personal vision, you throw away a part of yourself: your power. Giving up means giving away your power, and the farmer gave his power to the most unworthy subjects, friends who had laughed at him. Know your priorities.

> A year had passed, and now the trees were in bloom. There were flowers on the branches everywhere and the trees were truly beautiful. When one farmer saw the beautiful flowers, he thought they were the fruit. He bit into one and spat it out. It tasted terrible! This wasn't the beautiful fruit the stranger had brought to the village. He couldn't believe he had worked for so long, only to grow the wrong thing. Instead of an apple tree, he had grown a flower tree. He felt betrayed, used, and unforgiving. He tore off all the flowers, kicked the tree, and walked away forever.

Another sad ending because of impatience. The fourth farmer's impatience was a result of not understanding that growth usually comes in stages. This farmer didn't realize that out of the flowers come the fruit! He impatiently destroyed an important part of the fruit's development process. Are you that kind of farmer? Do you become frustrated and give up too easily? Or are you willing to be aware and alert so that you know when you've reached just a stage or plateau in your growth?

True enough, the flowers aren't good to eat. True enough, halfway to your goal isn't being there. But since flowers are a necessary part of the growing process, they can be used for just what they are — something beautiful that can be simply admired and enjoyed until later development brings the fruit. Sometimes you will have to rely on your intelligence to realize that you haven't failed, but rather that you are in a stage of growth that will develop further. Don't give up your aims until you've made an effort to thoroughly analyze where you are.

You didn't become an adult immediately after you were born. You went through many stages in the process. You didn't necessarily know when you were five years old where you would be when you were ten. You didn't know at ten where you would be at twenty. Just so, when you set out to change your life, you may not have a total overview of the events leading you to a certain outcome. So don't give up merely because you don't yet see yourself where you want to be. Every event in your life is teaching you something. To take the straightest path to your goal, make use of every little bus stop along the way.

Think of the biblical story of Joseph, whose brothers were jealous of him and, during a journey, abandoned him and left him to die. Worse, he eventually landed in prison and became a slave. Do you think he "knew" that these events were leading him to a position of political power in Egypt? Not very likely. More likely he was probably tempted to be angry, resentful, and unforgiving. After all, he had everything taken from him — his family, his wealth, his freedom. Yet, all along the way, through everything that happened to him, he remained loyal to his integrity and inner worth. No matter where he was, he expressed positive inner qualities, and his unique talents finally raised him to a position of power (serving as the right-hand assistant to Pharaoh). Unfortunate events he experienced were all leading somewhere, and fortunately, he did not indulge in impatient resentment. He held onto his integrity until a good end was reached.

Likewise, wherever you are right now, concentrate more on developing positive thoughts and feelings than on your actual circumstances. Keep your vision, and develop the mental traits that will get you where you want to be. Your circumstances will change as a result. Don't mistake stages of growth for the end result.

> Years passed and three farmers persevered. They had braved all the difficulties, and now their trees were bearing fruit. High in the boughs of their trees they could see the beautiful red fruit, just as they'd dreamed. But the problem was, they couldn't reach it.
>
> One farmer grabbed a nearby stick and decided he would knock his apples out of the tree. He swung at the branches, and beat all the apples out of the tree. Later, as he collected them, he saw how bruised and broken they were. As he bit into them, their sweetness was mixed with dirt and gritty pieces of rock. He felt disappointed and unfulfilled with such unpleasing fruit.

You've set out on a path toward a certain goal; you haven't quite arrived, so you become impatient and do something — anything — to try to make it happen. But this kind of impatience usually backfires in some way, just like the farmer's impatience. His failure was a result of being too impetuous, which is the wrong use of will power. He tried to force the outcome when he came upon a seemingly insurmountable obstacle. When you trust your Silent Master to bring about a certain manifestation, and you begin to see the results, you must keep trusting all the way to the end. This will sometimes require some patient listening on your part, a willingness to let your Silent Master give you direction when necessary.

Instead of realizing that getting the apples down was another stage of the process, and that waiting patiently for an intelligent way to do so was yet another stage, the farmer impetuously jumped in and used unintelligent "force." This is the wrong use of self-will, which will likely destroy what you have built. True will, as it comes from your Silent Master, is intelligent and effective when expressed, and produces harmony. True self-will is a result of listening to the inner voice of your Silent Master as it guides and protects you and leads you into harmonious action. If the farmer had taken the time to patiently listen within, a perfectly suitable solution to his problem would have appeared, and he would have enjoyed the fruits of his labors. Let yourself be guided when necessary.

Another farmer looked up at his red apples and began to savor all the hard work he'd put into them. He congratulated himself on all the sacrifices he had made — all the sweat and toil. He decided to lie down under the tree with his mouth open and wait for those sweet apples to drop into his mouth. He waited, and waited, and waited . . . and finally, a big deep red apple fell into his mouth. Quickly he bit into it, but to his surprise it was mushy and rotten inside and a huge worm crawled out as he looked at it. He regretted that he had wasted his time and felt cheated, having nothing but rotten apples to show for all his efforts.

Just as the fifth farmer shows us the wrong use of self-will, this farmer shows us the wrong use of patience. Patience does not mean that we expect our goal to be handed to us on a silver platter if we just wait long enough. This farmer celebrated a victory of the wrong thing at the wrong time, and therefore missed his true victory. He became a little too self-satisfied and smug by praising himself for his hard work, without realizing he needed to *do something* about the results of his hard work. It's true he successfully grew the apples, and that was a fine accomplishment, but it wasn't the real victory. The real victory would be to harvest the apples, and put them to use. Isn't that why they were grown? The farmers' goal was to harvest and eat the apples.

When you have a specific goal, you must recognize the moment of your true victory. For example, let's say you desire to heal a broken relationship. You work hard to gain more purity and understanding about your true self. Finally, you realize that you have learned many new concepts and ideas, and have released many bad habits. In fact, you have changed for the better. This is a great accomplishment, but it isn't the ultimate goal. Simply patiently waiting for the broken relationship to heal will most likely be totally ineffective. Instead, at this point, you need to actively use what you have learned. Then a total victory can be won. Recognize your true victory.

The last farmer was very small. He looked up at the tree and saw all the beautiful fruit. His heart beat with happiness and great anticipation as he looked at the victory within his reach. The harvest had come at last. But he didn't know how he was going to get the fruit down. He walked around the tree looking for a way, and then tried climbing the tree. He pulled himself up the tree trunk, but a little way up he slipped and fell. So close! He felt a little fear. Would he fail now? After coming so close to victory, would he fail now?

But he didn't listen to this fear. He picked himself up and tried again. Over and over he tried climbing the tree, and each time he fell down.

He began to wonder if perhaps he could not reach his goal. Perhaps it was impossible, he thought. Perhaps the victory he anticipated was all an illusion! Perhaps he should just give up. His heart sank.

But the thought of the apples just barely within his reach drove him on. He made another attempt, and another and another.

And then! Finally, stretched out on the highest branch, reaching just a little farther, stretching every muscle in his body, he could just feel the skin of the fruit. But could he reach any farther? In the next second, the apple was in his hand.

Think about this moment! After all those years, all his work, all his patience, he finally had the fruit in his hand: the biggest, reddest, and most beautiful apple he had ever seen! With an enormous sense of pride and accomplishment, he bit into it, and was filled with peace, harmony, and joy. In that moment, all the hardships he had endured, all the hours of work and effort, were worth it a million times over. The quiet love and joy he felt, the bliss, the peace and serenity he found within him was beyond any price.

This farmer used patience correctly. He waited patiently through all the small steps of the process, he remained loyal to his goal, he kept his priorities straight, he didn't mistake any stage of the process as being the end, he let himself be guided regarding how to get the apples down, and he certainly recognized what his true victory would be. This farmer also did one more thing: he persevered until the goal was in his hand the way he had desired.

Is this the kind of farmer you have proved to be? If so, I hope you are celebrating!

"It's not over 'til it's over." Nowhere is this truth clearer than for athletes who compete in the Olympic Games. Since the abilities of the Olympic athletes are so competitively similar, often the winner leads by a fraction of a second. In track competitions we see instances where a runner behind the likely winner suddenly pulls out and overtakes that person, winning the event by less than an inch. How important it is to persevere with all your commitment until the very end! Olympic athletes know all too well that, at the end of the race, letting up just a little can cost them a medal. In the same way, you too must persevere with full commitment until you reach your goal. The seventh farmer was not defeated by last-minute difficulties. He persevered until the apple was in his hand.

The rewards of remaining loyal until you arrive at your goal go beyond just obtaining the goal itself. Every time you win — even something small — or overcome a weakness or conquer a limitation, you make your true self more real and powerful in your life. This growth creates more growth and more challenges that bring out even more of your potential. And where does it all end? In greater *freedom* for you. The result of continuing self-discovery is the power to be more free.

The Right Use of Patience Promotes Victory

In the apple tree story we saw how the farmers started out doing everything right. They all had a specific goal that was reachable, they were enthusiastic and committed, and they all even visualized the desired outcome. They didn't just dream of their success; they took good action to set their goal in motion. Nothing should have hindered the manifestation for each, but, unfortunately, six of them at various stages became victims of their own impatient, undisciplined thinking.

But when you act as the seventh farmer did, you are well on your way to our ultimate goal of freedom!

PRACTICE

ONE

As we discussed, rebirth happens every moment you change in a positive way. When you express negative qualities, or when someone expresses them to you, you have an opportunity, even then, to put your own original Love into action. You have an opportunity to discard the negativity, and replace it with the truth about your real self. Look back over the past week and think of situations where you expressed negativity. There may be many or few. Instead of criticizing yourself for feeling and acting the way you did, look at an alternative action you could have taken in each situation. Jot down your responses this way:

"I felt jealousy in this situation and I reacted by.... Instead I could have ... and both of us would have felt better."

Or, "I felt anger when that person spoke to me harshly and I reacted by.... Instead, I could have said or done ... and we might have avoided the conflict."

Notice that the purpose of this exercise is not to prove you were wrong to have the negative emotion, but rather to show how a positive action or shift in attitude can help eliminate the cause of the negativity, and promote a new and different self-concept.

TWO

Try this exercise before you go to sleep, when you're relaxed and your mind is free. Imagine that you are an energy broadcasting station. Perhaps you can see yourself as a sphere of light, or perhaps your energy is invisible. However you do it, in this state you now have the ability to broadcast a message to anyone and everyone you choose in your present environment. You're going to let them know of your new goals, your new self-concept, or your new path. Look at your parents, for instance, with your new energy "eyes." Begin speaking to them, no matter what you see them doing, and know that your message is surrounding them and will be heard in some way. Tell them what kind of person you are and what you would like to bring to them and to the world. Tell them what you hope to do in life and what you need from them to help you do it. Broadcast to any friends or associates who also need to hear your message. This exercise is a form of visualization that actually helps create the life you're "broadcasting."

MEDITATION

Right now, I can express my Silent Master. Today, and every day, I can express more of my true self. Love within me is showing me true desires and true directions that bring me peace and joy and harmony. I am one with the Love of my Silent Master, so I can hear the voice of Love talk to me every moment, guiding me with true thoughts, ideas, and attitudes that help me create my greatest good. I willingly let go of every trait and every desire that is not my true self. I let go of every person, place, or thing that is not part of my true being and my true purpose. I can allow pure Love to shine through me and attract everything good to me. The potential for everything that I need to fulfill myself is within me now, and I am allowing Love, my creative energy, to bring it to me in the right way at the right time.

CHAPTER SIX

FREEDOM:
TAKING ACTION!

SILENT MASTER IMAGE V

YOU HAVE THE POWER
TO FULFILL YOUR DREAMS

Your Silent Master is completely aware, infinitely intelligent, and ready to give you all the insight, information, and direction you need to fulfill your dreams, ambitions, and goals. In fact, this Consciousness is the Source of all your true desires.

The whole point of discovering your real self — your Silent Master — is to be able to live free. So congratulations! You're living in a universe where freedom can be yours. Are you celebrating yet? If you aren't, maybe it hasn't become clear what freedom can mean to you personally. Have you been working on purifying and increasing your energy? Have you examined your life and prepared for the rebirth into freedom that rightfully belongs to you? Freedom is waiting for you right now. What action are you going to take to make it yours?

WHAT IS FREEDOM?

To me, one of the most perfect pictures of freedom is nature in the wild. Birds are free to fly wherever their instincts take them, to the highest mountain or to the water's edge. Bears, rabbits, deer, creatures of all names and sizes freely roam the land, each finding their food and shelter in their own individual way. Animals freely express their unique individuality. No animal tries to be like another. Mountain lions don't try to live like deer or eat their food. Rabbits don't try to hibernate like bears. All animals take their individuality for granted, "trusting" that nature provides everything necessary to fulfill their every need.

And the elements of nature are also free and joyous, expressing and contributing their gifts abundantly. The sun shines faithfully and warmly no matter what happens on the planet below. Rivers flow through their native surroundings bringing food for life. And beauty is everywhere. The clouds, winds, rainbows, butterflies, light filtered through the forest trees — all come together in a beautiful picture of harmony.

You are a part of all this! Freedom, beauty, and originality for you is exactly the same as for nature's beings and elements. You are an original! An individual, unique and special. You have your own talents and abilities, and don't have to imitate anyone else, or want what they have. You have your own special purpose. To discover your Silent Master is to realize that you have the power to create your own freedom. Living free means you put your freedom into action. You are the one in charge of the direction of your life. You don't let life happen to you. You don't let yourself be a victim.

Here on earth you live with many other people in many other nations. Since you can't control everything that happens in the world, freedom means that you control how you respond to the world. You control who you are, what you think and how you feel, and that shapes everything you experience. Freedom means you express your power to realize your goals and desires, so that nothing can take away your natural joy to be alive.

You are free when you can be the purity of yourself, no matter what happens — to you or to the world — and when you allow the purity of yourself to shine under all circumstances. The light of your own energy can chase away any darkness for you and promote healing and the solving of problems that confront you. You are your true creative self, and you create your own freedom by using your power to develop, protect, and express your life on your terms.

Freedom does not mean being free from adversity or difficulty. Freedom is the knowledge that you have the power to conquer adversity and difficulty. If you could ask any animal living free in the animal kingdom, they would tell you that they aren't free from "trouble." Predators are everywhere, and life is a daily challenge. But all animals were born with instincts to protect them, and were given special talents and abilities to help them stay alive and pursue their lives in freedom. It is the same for you. Living with over four billion other people, you will not be entirely free from trouble of many kinds. But the wisdom, intelligence, and creative power of your Silent Master is with you always to guide, protect, and support you. Freedom is knowing you are connected to this power source and that you can put it into action to conquer adversity.

You, and you alone, have the power to make yourself free, because taking charge of your life is a choice. You have within you right now your Silent Master consciousness, the creative Life Force of the universe. All you need do is choose to discover it. And then there's only one more step needed to complete your freedom: *Take action!*

READY FOR FREEDOM?
THEN GET READY TO TAKE ACTION

So many times I see students go to lectures, read books, take classes, and become really excited about a new goal. They talk about it, and talk about it some more. And then pretty soon they're couch potatoes again, in front of the television, staring with glazed eyes, mouth watering from watching fast food and beer commercials, and the only action they're taking is through a traffic jam to the refrigerator instead of taking action for their lives.

You've heard the expression, "Nothing succeeds like success." Here's another: "Nothing changes you like change." When you are finally ready to claim your freedom, when you're really ready to stop being a victim and take charge of your life, you are ready to make a change. Change means to take action — not to talk about it, not to give up after an enthusiastic start, not to hold back in fear, but to actually do something.

Making changes helps set you free by opening up many more alternatives and options for you. A person who knows just one way of doing something, just one way of being, is not as free as the person who can choose from many options.

Some of the actions you will need to take involve making changes that encourage you to look at additional options.

Are you willing to start making some changes? Are you willing to take even some small actions to start creating your freedom? Sometimes after students set goals, they feel they don't know where to start. When they ask me about it, I tell them to start anywhere. . . . Just start! Start with the following actions:

Set Realistic Goals

In order to produce the kind of big change that makes you free from being a victim, start with little changes. Some people make the mistake of expecting too much from themselves, then get easily disappointed and give up. If you've spent the last twenty years handling all your conflicts with anger, you will not be a tranquil "saint" tomorrow. It may take a lot of time and work to remove that habit. So, even though you set the elimination of anger as a goal, you also set a smaller realistic goal: *Today, during the two hours when I visit my mother-in-law, I will practice listening to her and responding with love no matter what she says.* Or, you could set a goal like this: *Today, I will go to the person I threatened and yelled at, apologize, and negotiate a good solution to our problem.* Practicing these small changes eventually produces the big change: one day you realize you don't respond with anger anymore.

Can you imagine the freedom that would bring? If you remember the last time you were really angry at someone, you will realize how good it would feel never to have anger anymore. Do you realize how the person you were angry at had complete control over you at the time — control that you allowed? You were not free. You let another person determine that your throat would tighten, that your heart would pound and feel explosive. That individual determined you would be out of control, and perhaps do something hurtful or violent. You let yourself be a victim. Do you really want someone else to determine how you feel and act?

Now imagine that you have eliminated this destructive reaction. You use your power to take control of yourself. You take charge. You decide what you will feel. No matter what someone else does, you decide how you respond, and once you decide, you never again feel this terrible anger. You find that your calm and loving manner actually works to remove the conflict and restore harmony. How free you would be! And this is just one little aspect of freedom.

But if you've been angry for twenty years, this freedom won't come overnight. You will have to practice, not just think about it, but practice, in every little way you can find.

Turn Off Negative Inner Dialog

Have you ever made a point of listening to what you think? Try it the next time you are alone, when you dress in the morning, or take a shower, or shave. How much of your thinking is really negative: "I can't do that. . . . I wish I was strong. . . . I'm so lazy. . . . I don't have any energy. . . . I'm so weak. . . . I hate the way I look. . . . I'm so bored. . . . I hate doing this. . . . This won't work out. . . . I'll never get that. . . ." Even if you don't hear yourself thinking in words, what silent feelings do you carry around in your neutral state? Are you mainly peaceful and optimistic? Or do you feel constant dread and anxiety? Chances are you'll find that much of the time, you are feeling or talking to yourself in a negative way.

Many times when I'm trying to encourage and energize people, I hear them say, "Well, maybe I could do that,' or "I guess I can," or "I think I might." This kind of language indicates how weak they are in their thinking. Making a change is going to require a much stronger commitment than "maybe," "I guess," or "I might."

Since this kind of negativity is so familiar, you may not see how destructive it is. Since this constant inner dialog has been a habit for so long, it now operates all by itself unconsciously. That means you will have to break the habit *consciously.*

Almost everyone is in front of a mirror for a period of time every day, so an exercise I give is to ask students to deliberately carry on a positive dialog while they look at themselves in the mirror. You say, "I *can* do this or that.... I *will* accomplish ... I *know* I have ... I *do* express ... I *am* a good ... I *am* a beautiful ..." and so on. See how quickly this dialog energizes you and produces a natural smile and a feeling of well being. Don't be afraid to like yourself! How easily we say we love apple pie, and we love going to the races, and we love our children and our spouses. But how easily do you say you love yourself? Try saying it often. Someday you will come to believe it, and then you'll know the quiet inner warmth and joy that comes when you love, support, and trust yourself.

Use this mirror exercise to become familiar with yourself, so that you don't feel like a stranger to yourself. If your negative inner dialog has become so familiar that you don't even notice it, you may have a lot of work to do to get in touch with your true feelings and desires.

Change Your Posture

Hardly anything indicates self-esteem and self-confidence better than posture does. People who don't like themselves or who don't believe in themselves show it in their poor, slouchy posture. People who are radiating positive energy, who know who they are and where they're going, stand up and walk straight and tall. People who have given up will show it not only in their posture, but in their eyes. They look down, avoid eye contact with others, shift their gaze all around as if they can't focus anywhere, and don't have that sparkle and light that shines in the eyes of happy people. Remember, body and mind are one. People whose eyes are always shifting around are not focused in their thinking. Their eyes show it. They don't have a strong, focused sense of who they are, and they feel weak and insecure.

Even if you don't have a lot of self-esteem yet, you can start to change your physical self to look like you do. Since your body and mind are connected, you can encourage your mind to change by changing your body. While you look in the mirror, deliberately breathe in and raise yourself up straight. Look yourself in the eye, and get used to how that feels. Automatically, you will look more confident, and if you can become more aware of your posture throughout the day — sitting, standing, and walking — you will begin to actually feel more confident. Why? Because controlling your posture is one small way of taking charge. You actually take charge of the space you're standing in by "filling it" with yourself. Poor posture and slouching is body language that says: "I'm small and insignificant, so I shouldn't be here and take up any room." Standing tall is body language that says, "I matter, I count, I'm important, and I deserve to be here and take up space." When you have this belief, it will help create situations where you are important, where you do matter. So, let a physical action — having better posture — help create a positive mental attitude.

Change Your Appearance and Habits

Nothing changes you like change. Making even small changes in your appearance or physical habits sends messages to your whole personality, messages like, Change is okay. . . . Change can be fun. . . . Change can bring good results. These messages encourage even more change, and as a result, you may find yourself transforming fairly rapidly.

Just as you generally repeat your familiar inner dialog, you tend to repeat physical habits. In the same way you help to change mental attitudes by changing your posture, you can also do the same by changing even small physical habits.

Have you had long hair for the past ten years? To some extent, your long hair is a picture of the past. Consider changing your hairstyle. Cut it, even a little bit. That's something that can't hurt, because no matter what, it grows again. But removing the old picture of the past helps you focus on the new.

Do you always wear navy blue or gray or black? Try another color. Try different colors in your shoes, your pants, your shirts, your dresses, or your lipstick. Color affects your energy in different ways; experiment with the effects of different colors on your energy and personality. In addition to differences you may discover, you may also find that people respond to you differently when you wear certain colors.

Do you always eat the same food? Try something new. (Again, it can't hurt because you don't have to eat it again.) But at least you will have tried something new and you will have expanded your experience.

What if you find that you like the changes? In that case, you've broadened yourself, and have given yourself the freedom of having more alternatives and options in your life.

Be Willing to Take Chances

If you are not enthusiastic and excited about making some of these changes, don't be surprised. One of the reasons you haven't made these changes before is that it's a little bit scary to give up what's familiar. Making a change is taking a chance, right? You don't know what will happen. You don't know how others will respond. You don't have any experience with this new way of doing or being or thinking. But taking chances is what builds confidence. And confidence is what helps propel you along the self-discovery process.

Think back to when you first learned something new — like riding a bicycle. You probably were afraid and lacked confidence. Standing on the sidewalk talking about how to get on and move the pedals and stay balanced wouldn't have done much good at all. You had to get on the bicycle and try it until you discovered you could actually do it. *Then* you had confidence. Just so, if you stand around waiting to have the confidence to do something, it most likely will never come. Do something first, and then you gain confidence!

Express Yourself Clearly

One very positive way of taking charge of your life is to assume the power to express yourself. Become willing to say in some way, I *want*, or I *need*, or I *am*.

Many people never start on a good path to a goal because they can't assert themselves. They don't feel good enough — or aware enough — to say I want this, or I need that. Instead they have a fuzzy self-image, and rarely make good decisions, never make any long-term plans, never know who they really are, and as a result, never assert and express themselves.

Learning to express yourself is important. Victims don't do this. In fact, one of the most common characteristics of victims is that they just silently accept everything that happens to them without making a stand. Making a stand does not mean aggressively provoking a confrontation. It just means knowing who you are and what you want or what you expect. Victims are victims because they believe they can't act. (And people who provoke fights are often those who feel they can't take constructive action to get what they want, so conflict becomes their only tactic.)

When you know who you are and what you want, you have a pretty good understanding of your priorities. When you know your priorities, you tend to take intelligent action that leads you away from distractions, obstructions, and conflicts. You're focused. And when you're focused, your direction stays clear. You know with certainty what you want, what you need, or what you expect, because you express it.

Clearly and strongly expressing yourself helps you stay on your path. When something happens that stands in your way, don't behave like a victim and give up. Take responsibility to get yourself around the obstacle and continue on your way. Again, only people who know clearly who they are and where they're going can stay focused. Start to know now what your priorities are and express them without fear.

Here are some ways to help you stay focused.

Clearly Identify Your Goals and Plans

Perhaps you aren't a natural list maker, but many people are comfortable with lists, and use them in different ways. People walk around the supermarket with shopping lists, and you see people writing their "to do" list every day in the office. They are using a good method to protect them from getting distracted, forgetting or losing sight of their goal.

Even if this is not a common habit of yours, putting your goals in writing is one of the clearest ways of focusing your intentions. When you commit your goals to writing, you take one step away from thinking about doing something, and one step toward actually doing it.

It's all too easy to have general intentions like, I'd like to have a better life. . . . I'd like more financial freedom. . . . I'd like a bigger place to live. . . . But thoughts like these don't get off the ground very easily. Wishes don't have the power of goals. Good intentions and wishes must be translated into specific goals in order to take form. "A better life" could be translated into many specific goals. Owning a dog might be a way to a better life for someone, but getting a boat to pursue an interest in sailing might be someone else's idea of a better life, or getting married, or living in a different country. Have you thought about what specifically would make your life better? Don't be surprised if you don't know. Many of us are so used to thinking in an unfocused way about our lives that we really aren't familiar with our true desires. Think about it now. What do you really want? What would make you feel fulfilled and happy? What do you need to do to get it?

Once you do know what you want, then set a goal with a specific outcome. "I'd like more financial freedom" needs to be stated this way: "I want my income to increase by $20,000 next year." When you are specific, you can more easily design a plan to meet that goal. "I will reach that goal by doing the following things to my business." Or, "I will reach that goal by selling my house and investing elsewhere." You would probably take very different actions if your goal were to have only an additional $1,000, so it's important to know exactly what you want in order to take appropriate action. Even if your goal is more intangible, such as "I want to eliminate anger as a way of life," or "I wish to express more love to my family," you still need a plan that consists of some specific actions you will take.

Feed Your Goals in Specific Ways Every Day

Hopefully by now you have some kind of list that indicates your goals. It is important to keep these goals alive and well in your thoughts and feelings every day. Feeding your goals energizes them, giving them the mental energy they need to take form.

When you stand in front of the mirror every morning and carry on an inner negative dialog, you're feeding negative goals. Is that really what you want to take form? I think not. So in addition to turning off negative inner dialog, you need to feed your positive goals. One way to do this is to review your goals every morning before you start your day. When we wake up, there is ordinarily a routine pressure to numbly jump up and somehow get out the door to work.

Instead, you can plan to get up and consciously connect with the universe before rushing into the work day. If you have a backyard, go outside and feel yourself among the plants and trees and birds, feel the breeze, and experience the light of the rising sun. Or, at least imagine these things, or spend a few minutes in quiet meditation feeling the peace of your Silent Master.

Then, go over your list of goals, either mentally or by writing them. Perhaps some of your goals are to express more affection to your spouse ... to show more patience with a difficult co-worker ... to get your exercise hour in to-day ... to stay on your diet ... to find a solution to the prob-lem of how to buy a new house ... to spend more time with the children. . . . What's important to you? What do you want to accomplish? It can be short-term or long-term.

When your goals are clear and focused in your mind, the next step is to spend your day in charge of these goals. Instead of going about the day waiting to see what will hap-pen *to* you, spend the day *acting on* your goals. When you take charge of your day, you take charge of your life. Don't wait for something unusual to happen in order to express patience and kindness, for example. Do it from the start.

Even with planning, there is always a tendency for your best intentions to slip away. That's why I also suggest you keep your goals visible. Put a sign in your bedroom, your kitchen, your car, beside your desk, anywhere at all giving you a friendly reminder of an important goal. Maybe your sign says, Remember to Smile, or Anger Hurts Only Yourself; Love Instead, or Get Thin and Win, or whatever you want to work on.

Change Your Environment

Just as changing your posture, your appearance, and your physical habits can help change your thinking, changing your environment can make a powerful contribution toward your transformation. A new environment can help free you from the past.

Environment is a pretty big concept. It covers everything from the place where you live and the place where you work to the places where you socialize and even the relationships you're involved in. How much of that you need to consciously change is a matter of judgment. Eventually, as you change, your environment will have a corresponding change. When you are no longer addicted to alcohol, for instance, you simply won't go to the bars where you used to hang out. When you complete your night school training in electronics, you will leave your present unsatisfactory work environment. Although these natural changes will occur, it's important to look at areas of your environment that would best be changed by you now.

Human beings are conditioned by elements of their environment. If you live in a house where you've had many destructive conflicts with someone, the house itself is a constant reminder of the conflicts. Subconsciously, the negative energy remains with you as long as the same sights, sounds, and smells surround you. Your subconscious is such an effective record keeper and tape recorder that you may even find yourself feeling mildly irritated or anxious when you see someone else's couch or table that is similar to one in your house.

Putting yourself in a new house, in a different location, with different colors, with as much different furniture as you can obtain would be an ideal action to take after leaving a long, troublesome relationship. You would give yourself a good opportunity to really let go of the past and to welcome new feelings and sensations.

It's the same with some relationships. Have you noticed that your behavior changes when you are around certain acquaintances? With some people you tend to be honest, out-going, and expressive; with others you tend to be self-indulgent or frivolous. Perhaps around some others you are insecure, or insincere and somewhat phony. If so, ask your-self if you really want to keep those relationships that encourage you to express qualities you're trying to eliminate. If you're trying to stop drinking or using drugs, do you really want to be around people who do these things?

You can say that such relationships are a test, and that you should be able to be yourself no matter who you're with. That's true, but that's not the way it works all the time. Even if you maintain your integrity in an environment where peo-ple pressure you to be frivolous and self-indulgent, they'll probably want to stop seeing you if you don't conform. If they can accept your different way of life, that's fine. But be prepared that, as you change, you may not be able to keep the same relationships — in fact, you may not want to keep them. If you have finally lost all the weight you wanted, do you really want to mingle in groups who socialize only by eating? Select your environment carefully to help keep your commit-ment pure and strong.

In short, you must always use your power of choice to protect your freedom. When you look at an element in your environment and decide to eliminate it, you're saying very powerfully, I have the power of choice. This is not *who I am. I choose another environment because that is who I am.* When you do this, you are taking charge of your life in a big way.

Use Your Power of Awareness

When you make a decision to change your environment, you've done something very important. You've used your power of awareness. Many people remain in destructive envi-ronments for a long time because they're not aware how destructive those environments are. They feel familiar, so they feel comfortable. Your awareness increases as you purify your thoughts and feelings. The more you become your true self, the clearer undesirable elements become to you.

When you stop using drugs, you don't stay away from people who use them because you're afraid, but because you choose to stay out of environments that are negative and unproductive.

It's like this: When you're walking down the street and see dog excrement blocking your path, your awareness enables you to go around it. You don't go around it because you're afraid of it. But why go through it? If you do, it will get pretty messy and cause you a lot of work and effort afterward. How much more intelligent to just be thankful for your awareness, and take the extra steps to avoid it. You are living free when you know how to be aware of negative situations that can be avoided.

Be Aware of Beauty

One way to further develop your awareness is to practice using it to appreciate the beauty around you. Appreciation and gratitude are ways of acknowledging that something is present and real. When you acknowledge and appreciate beauty, you are making it real in your world. And making beauty real in your world is another way of taking charge of your life. Because you can see beauty everywhere, let this perception set you free from being a victim of self-imposed ugliness, gloom, and depression.

Those times that I've enjoyed the mountains and blue sky of the wilderness I've always had the same thought: There is no artist who can create this kind of beauty. No photograph, no painting can match this. The more I stand there and just *appreciate*, the more I feel as though I'm making my own music. That's why I tell people to "wake up and hear the music." Or, "wake up and make your own music!" What I'm telling them is to wake up and see how much there is to appreciate. So many people are victims of negative thinking and dark emotions because they don't realize how much there is to see and feel that can create natural, effortless, positive feelings.

It's easy to experience the beauty of nature if you can get away to do it. In the city, appreciation is a little tougher. But aside from the beautiful architecture, gardens, and parks, there is much more to appreciate, even in the city.

Cities are centers of technology. Our lives today are dependent on the technology we have created. Think about those times when your water had to be turned off for a day, or when the electricity went out, or when you had to do without your car. To some extent your routine life just stopped. One very good way to practice appreciation is to look at the everyday items you have around you and think about the creative ideas that went into them. We were given pleasure, leisure, and ease from someone's creativity.

For instance, I am still fascinated by an ordinary washing machine. The way the water comes and goes, the way the soap and bleach are dispensed, the way the clothes agitate — all this is really a great achievement we take for granted. On laundry day, if all you think of is drudgery and boredom, try curing your blues by appreciating the virtues of your washing machine. If that doesn't help, then try the alternative that many people have. Pick up your laundry basket and your soap, and walk to the nearest river or lake. Hopefully, it won't be more than a couple of miles each way, depending on where you live. And hopefully, the river water will be clean. (Be sure and take another container for washing the clothes so you don't soap up the river.) Then, by hand, wash all your laundry, and then wait for it to dry, since wet clothes are heavy to carry.

See what I mean — technology is something to appreciate even if you don't live in the heart of nature. But when I say to appreciate technology, this is not an invitation to disregard ecological needs. Unfortunately, technology has had a negative impact on the environment in many ways. We all need to be responsible for the ecology, and for contributing our part in saving the health and beauty of the Earth. But the wrong use of technology is not a reason to eliminate it. Instead, we can use better or different technological creativity to protect and improve the environment as we continue to grow.

You can also create beauty in your home. In my surroundings, for instance, I like to have beautiful things that are hand-made, because I know the creator could not produce them with anger or other bad feelings. Artists who create beauty are in a positive state of mind when they produce their work. When I have their work in my surroundings, not only do I have my own good feelings from appreciating the beauty, but also I have a symbol of the artists' positive energy as well.

The point is this: Always find something to appreciate — no matter what. Appreciation does wonders to keep your mind free from the heavy negativity that encloses you in limitation, fear, and oppression. You've seen those hot air balloons that rise so lightly? Appreciation is like the force that tosses out the weights that keep the balloons on the ground. Without those weights, the balloons rise naturally and freely. That's how you can be when you allow appreciation and gratitude to fill your heart and mind. Appreciation keeps you focused on good things, and this causes more good to manifest. In this way, you become free of the negative forms that have manifested from your negative and limited thoughts.

Look Within Your Own Mind
for Freedom and Happiness

Whatever your material goals are, the purpose of achieving any goal is to arouse the natural joy and happiness already within you. True happiness is feeling your own spiritual qualities, not limited, negative thoughts and feelings. True happiness is spiritual because it is never dependent on just material things or material success. There is great freedom when you know this because you can never lose your joy, never lose your power, never lose your happiness, no matter what your material circumstances are.

Remember the story of the apple farmer who succeeded? He got the apples, all right. But wasn't the real prize the peace and joy and fulfillment he felt? Even if his apple trees burned down the next day, would he still have that peace and joy and fulfillment? Yes! Why? Because the material apples were not the source of happiness. The farmer's success in growing the apples brought out the feelings of peace and joy already within him.

The apples were not the source of his happiness, but rather the means he used to find his own intangible feelings of happiness within. It wouldn't be wrong for the farmer to say something like this to the apple tree: "Thank you for this opportunity. Thank you for being here, and growing, and giving me this opportunity to practice disciplines I used to help you bring forth the apples. As a result, I now know I am a strong person with good qualities, and I am grateful for the peace and joy and contentment I have discovered within me. Now that I know I have this joy inside me, I know I will have it forever."

This is sometimes a hard lesson to learn. We strive so hard to acquire the material things and the material situations we think will make us happy. We really think this is what we need to do. But over and over again, we find that acquiring something material does not make us happy. In fact, after we get something, even if it's something we really wanted, we usually quickly move on to get something else. And each time, we never seem to get the final, lasting happiness that we desire. That's because we're looking in the wrong place when we look outside ourselves.

Happiness is already within! Material goals and material things are only ways of helping you discover your natural inner joy. When a victory brings you joy, it's up to you to keep it. Since your joy is not created only by material things, you don't lose your joy when you lose those material things. What freedom there is in this! Not only can you achieve your material goals, but you can also use them to help you realize your inner qualities — spiritual qualities of joy, peace, and harmony that can never be destroyed.

Here's a story I like to tell about inner happiness:

One day a king was contemplating the nature of happiness and decided to see if he could find the answer within his kingdom. He called his advisor and said, "I want you to go out into my kingdom in secret and see if you can find a household that is truly happy. If you can find one that is without care or worries, I will have learned much, and I will reward them."

First the advisor thought he would try a rich family. He went to a huge house with servants and all forms of luxuries. He managed to get a job inside so he could better observe, and he fully expected this family would be happy since they had everything they could want. But after a few days, he saw how unhappy they were. They were constantly worried about people trying to steal their money or take their belongings.

Next the advisor tried a family with a very good position in society and a high position in the government. They also were not as happy as he had anticipated, because they were always worried about spies and about losing their status or hurting their position.

The advisor then tried the household of the most beautiful woman in the kingdom. She had so many admirers, so many suitors, gifts, and expensive things that he was sure she must be very happy. But he soon found that she wasn't. She didn't know which person to marry, and she lived in constant fear of getting old and losing her beauty.

For months the advisor searched everywhere, and no matter how good the household looked from the outside, it was almost always full of somber fear, worry, and anxiety on the inside.

Finally, after he had exhausted almost all the households in the kingdom, the advisor came to a small house on the outskirts of town. It was a very poor-looking house, so he didn't even bother to look further for any happiness. Just as he was about to walk away, he heard an unexpected sound. It was laughter. He turned around and came close enough to look quietly through the window without being seen.

Inside the one-room house was the father, the mother, and their little child, all sitting on the floor. The parents were playing with their child and all three of them were loving and laughing without a care.

The advisor's heart grew warm and his weariness fell away as he watched them. He was amazed that this household with so little could be so happy. Then he heard the father say with a long sigh, "Oh, my son, there is nothing in the world that I want more than what I have. You are everything to me, and I am happy. But it would fill my heart with joy if only I could afford to buy you some new underwear."

The advisor couldn't believe his ears. Throughout the whole kingdom everyone was worried about so many things that were not even significant. Yet this poor family was happy even though they had a real need, something that everyone else took for granted.

The next day the advisor returned in a manner befitting his position, dressed in gold and silver and with all his servants and aides around him. Proudly he rode into the city where he'd found the happy household and told everyone of his mission. Many people recognized him as the stranger who'd asked so many questions.

He announced that he had selected the happiest household in the kingdom and that this household would be richly rewarded. Everyone waited breathlessly as the advisor got marched through the crowd to the poor family in the back. He smiled broadly as he reached within his cloak, and with a wink, brought out the most beautiful set of children's clothes you could imagine. Underwear included!

As this family shows us, joy is something that exists all by itself. The family was happy naturally, with or without material goods. Material objects were regarded as enhancements, not necessities, and so happiness can only be increased, not lost. You are really free when you find a natural joy within you and discover it is a part of you forever. Why? Because nothing can ever rob you of your joy, and your joy will never depend on particular circumstances for it to exist.

As an aspect of your Silent Master, joy is a creative attitude. Remember, body and mind are one. When you hold joy in your mind, you hold one of the positive feelings that helps you create beautiful free forms in your physical life. Just as Love creates loveliness, joy creates happiness that is seen in your relationships, your work, and your home.

Never Forget Your Connection

For all eternity, you will be one with the Life Force of the universe. Believe in yourself, your capability to perform and produce. Your Silent Master is your connection to the same source that created everything that exists. When you feel your Silent Master, you feel yourself as strong, pure, beautiful, and true. Feel yourself this way, feel powerful, and know you can achieve.

You're not alone. You know your Silent Master within you will create all solutions to your problems if you ask. Know this. If you are truly searching — body, mind, and spirit — you are not alone. Know that this wisdom within you has a quiet voice called intuition that will speak to you and guide you when you ask. You feel joy and rest and peace. Your connection brings you this quiet joy because you feel safe and secure being one with the source of all life.

You know that as you love and feel and desire with purity, you are co-creating your life with this creative Life Force that is your own mind. Be the warrior! Whatever happens, whatever appears to you, you have the infinite Life Force within you ready to bring healing, restoration, abundance, and beauty. Spread your wings!

It's your life and your world. You are an original, a special and unique gift to the universe, because there's only one of you. The universe needs you to be complete. It's time to stop living in fear, waiting, wishing, and hoping for something better. You are already at one with the creative force that brought you and the whole universe into being. Don't let anybody stand in your way. Don't let anybody clip your wings! Take action! You already have all the power you need in your thoughts and feelings to be and do and have everything you desire. Since you know this now, ignorance is not stopping you. Only laziness is. Only the habits of the past. Spread your wings!

You live in a wonderful time called *now*. In this moment, everything true about you is waiting to be recognized and expressed. Everything in the past is gone. Tomorrow will never come. There is always only now. You can take charge, take action, and create freedom for yourself.

Right here and right now let's start celebrating! Freedom is real. Freedom is possible. You have power, truth, beauty, and potential within you always waiting to be discovered, always waiting to be expressed. Brighter and more precious than diamonds, warm as the spring sun, and beautiful like spirals of galaxies sprinkled over this vast universe, your Silent Master awaits your return, so that together you will come forth as one radiant being in charge of your destiny.

What is stopping you? What is holding you back? You are free to be free! Spread your wings! Fly and be free!

MEDITATION

Right now, I set myself free from every thought, feeling, and action that is not my true self. I allow my joy, my love, my happiness to shine in me every moment unhindered by any-one or anything. My love and joy are creating loveliness, beauty, peace, and harmony in all my actions and in every place I go. The love of my Silent Master fills all space. I know my mind is free, my spirit is free, my love is free, and every-where I turn my love comes backs to me, showing me that Love is the energy of all manifestation.

ABOUT THE AUTHOR

Grandmaster Tae Yun Kim is the first woman in the history of Korean martial arts to earn the rank of Master. She is the only female Grandmaster, and is the founder of her own art, Jung SuWon. She began training at the age of seven, learning ancient methods of Gi-energy development in the solitude of the Korean mountains.

In her career, Grandmaster has smashed barriers of race, sex, and tradition. At less than five feet tall and weighing ninety pounds, she proved that it is not the size of one's body that counts, but the size of one's heart. She is now adored in the country that once spurned her, and is honored in her adopted land. She is reaping the rewards of more than forty years of patience, perseverance, and a positive approach to life.

Grandmaster lives her philosophy: celebrate every breath, every moment, every heartbeat. Her message is simple: What we generate from within, we receive. Knowing that we are all going to face obstacles and temptations, we have to learn to rejoice in the lessons of pain and hurt and suffering, to forcefully focus on the positive aspects of *every* situation, and to see the future good instead of dwelling on the negative.

All her life, Grandmaster has acted on that belief. She bears no malice toward those who mistreated her as a child. After all, they thought they were doing the right thing — it had never occurred to anyone in their culture that a female might belong in the martial arts. But Grandmaster's forgiveness and acceptance goes beyond that. Every day, Grandmaster *thanks* those who gave her such a hard time. She thanks them for giving her the opportunity to develop her strength and for the chance to learn the power of generating love every moment.

Perhaps it is this total love and forgiveness that makes her appear so radiant, so bubbling with life. Perhaps that is why people confuse her with a model or a movie star. After all, how could someone so glamorous and outgoing be a master of martial arts and meditation?

Or perhaps it is because she relishes a challenge, and just loves it when people tell her that something is impossible — because she is out to demonstrate that what appears to be impossible really is possible, if you believe in yourself, take charge with conviction in your heart, and refuse to be a copy of others' expectations.

For Grandmaster, "Be an Original" has the force of a moral imperative. It means being true to the dictates of your own heart and following your own dreams, instead of accepting a life that others have mapped out for you. To pursue her dreams, Grandmaster fought off a culture that said women should only cook and sew and farm, enter into an arranged marriage, and bear twelve sons. She faced peer pressure, ridicule, ostracism, and beatings. But she followed her vision, and she refused to become embittered.

On the physical side, her philosophy of not treating her body like a trash can has kept her strong, slim, and flexible. On the mental and spiritual side, her philosophy of not treating her *mind* like a trash can has kept her youthful, beautiful, and energetic. Today she not only enjoys success, but love and happiness as well. Grandmaster visibly demonstrates the value and the power of her teachings.

OTHER RESOURCES
BY GRANDMASTER TAE YUN KIM

Self-Development Programs

- *Self-Discovery Weekends:* Weekend Self-Development seminars held in the beauty and majesty of nature.

- *Intensive Programs:* This program is customized for people who wish to address a specific area in their self-development on a private or semi-private basis. Usually 1 to 2 weeks long.

- *Correspondence Programs:* These programs are specifically designed for people who cannot attend regular classes, and want to continue their learning. Usually taken after one of the courses above.

- *Seminars:* For companies or special interest groups. Available upon request. Custom tailored for specific needs.

- *Personal Consultation with Grandmaster Kim:* Private consultation one on one with Grandmaster Kim (in person or by phone) is available by appointment.

Meditation and Motivational Audio Tapes

- *Be Free* — Grandmaster leads you through a meditation exercise designed to dissolve self-destructive forces.

- *Rising Above* — Rise above and become the master of your life.

- *Be An Original* — This ancient meditation technique will help you tap into your true inner potential.

- *Ocean Magic* — Learn how to draw inspiration and energy from nature's forces.

- *Grandmaster's Song* — Soothing meditation music inspired by Grandmaster.

- *Personal Power* — A dynamic one-hour hour seminar with Grandmaster Tae Yun Kim on the topic of controlling your environment.

- *Ki Rhythm Energy Channeling Series* — The Energy Channeling Series is a collection of beautifully produced Vibrational Chants sung by Grandmaster Tae Yun Kim.

  Jung Shin Tong II — It is now time to spread your Rainbow Wings.

  Tae Yun — Give yourself permission to connect with your larger self.

  Song Bu — Calling the Creator as a child of God. Unconditional Love.

  Om — Universe Sound Vibration.

  Chu Yo Ho Hwa Yo — Trust, carry love and gratitude, experience letting go.

  Ha Nu Rey Gae Shin — Becoming a citizen of Heaven.

  Ki Do — Connecting with your Silent Master and with God.

Motivational Video Tapes

- *Shim Gong* — Outlines the Seven Steps to Inner Power and the integration of these concepts into our lives. Exciting action, beauty, and grace.

- *Hyung* — This video explains the inner meaning of Martial Art forms and how to apply them to your personal development.

- *Nae Gong* — Emphasizes the importance of mental discipline in our everyday life.

- *Ki Energy* — This video explains and demonstrates how to incorporate Ki Energy into every aspect of your daily life. Exercises, examples, and testimonials.

For more information, write to:

GRANDMASTER TAE YUN KIM

107 Minnis Circle, Milpitas, CA 95035

(408) 263-5425

If you enjoyed *The Silent Master*, we highly recommend the following books from New World Library:

Seven Steps to Inner Power by Grandmaster Tae Yun Kim. A guide for overcoming limitations, developing spiritual and mental power, and attaining mastery in life.

Creative Visualization by Shakti Gawain. This international bestseller with more than two million copies in print gives us easy and effective ways to use our imagination to create the lives we want.

Internal Power by Harold W. Becker. Using powerful visualizations and experiential exercises, the author reveals how to tap your internal power by using the energy of your thoughts to transform and energize your life.

The Perfect Life by Marc Allen. This powerful book shows you step by step how to map a course that moves you toward the realization of your dreams.

As You Think by James Allen. An updated and revised edition of *As a Man Thinketh,* this classic has inspired readers for nearly a century. (Available in hard cover, paperback and audio cassette.)

The Message of a Master by John McDonald. This inspiring book clearly shows us how we can harness the forces within to achieve health, vitality and prosperity.

New World Library is dedicated to publishing books and cassettes that help improve the quality of our lives.

For a catalog of our fine books and cassettes, contact:

New World Library
58 Paul Drive
San Rafael, CA 94903

Phone: (415) 472-2100
FAX: (415) 472-6131

Or call toll free:
(800) 227-3900